AN ANALYTICAL APPROACH TO

LINEAR APPLICATIONS:

Integrating Gospel Drumming into Your Grooves and Chops

Lang Zhao

VIOLET ANAMNESIS PUBLICATIONS
SAN DIEGO, CALIFORNIA

Copyright © 2016 Violet Anamnesis Publications.

All rights reserved. No part of this publication may be reproduced, distributed or transmitted in any form or by any means, including photocopying, recording, or other electronic or mechanical methods, without the prior written permission of the publisher, except in the case of brief quotations embodied in critical reviews and certain other noncommercial uses permitted by copyright law. For permission requests, write to the publisher, addressed "Attention: Permissions Coordinator," at the address below.

Violet Anamnesis Publications
11880 Bernardo Terrace Suite B
San Diego, CA/92128
www.violetanamnesispublications.com

Cover Design by Nyla McDaniel (Flipping Frowns)

Content co-designed by: Ziyin Zhao

Assisted and coordinated by: Ziyin Zhao

Proofread by: David Montoya, Ziyin Zhao

Video Demonstrated by: Henry McDaniel IV (Stanley Clarke/George Duke band, Big Sean, MacBear)

Author photo by: Ekaterina Gorbacheva

"Drive It" Track composed by: Kaz Rodriguez

An Analytical Approach to Linear Applications / Lang Zhao. —1st ed.
ISBN 978-1-944213-27-5

Contents

Introduction 7

Part 1: Preparations 10

   Session 1: Proper Sound 13

   Session 2: Training on Timing and Note Placement Accuracy: The Metronome 21

      2.1• Note Placement 22

      2.2• Consistency and Micro-Approach 23

      2.3• Time Feel Stability and Macro-Approach 26

   Session 3: Base Drum Placements 29

      3.1• Counting System 30

      3.2• Metronome System 31

      3.3• Bass Drum Placement, Hi-Hat Foot Control, and Basic 4-way Coordination 33

Part 2: Practical Applications of Grooves and Chops 38

   Session 4: Linear Applications and Demo Analysis 41

      4.1• DEMO 44

      4.2• Groove Construction 51

         4.2.1. Define the Skeleton and the Subdivision of Flow 52

         4.2.2. Define a Skeleton 52

         4.2.3. Sonic Vocabulary Elements 53

      4.3• Chops Construction 58

         4.3.1. Chops as Fills 58

         4.3.2. Chops Inside of the Grooves under the Musical Content 60

         4.3.3. Chops as Long Passages of Improvisation 64

Session 5: A Word on Practice 69

Session 6: Linear Coordination Part 1: Double-Note Interdependence 73

- 6.1 • Fundamental Sticking 74
- 6.2 • Orchestration 74
  - 6.2.1. Alternative Hand Patterns RL or LR 75
  - 6.2.2. Double Stroke Sticking RR or LL 75
- 6.3 • Grid 76
- 6.4 • Accents and Highlights 76
  - 6.4.1. Accents in Doubles 76
  - 6.4.2. Flams in Alternative Strokes 77
  - 6.4.3. Flams in Double Strokes 78
  - 6.4.4. Double Flams 78
  - 6.4.5. Orchestrating Flams 79
  - 6.4.6. Cymbal Highlights 80
- 6.5 • Rate Changing Grid 81

Session 7: Linear Coordination Part 2: Single-Note Interdependence 83

- 7.1 • Fundamental Sticking 84
  - 7.1.1. Fundamental Sticking 84
  - 7.1.2. Grid for Fundamental Stickings 85
- 7.2 • Basic Groupings 87
  - 7.2.1. Four-Note Grouping 87
  - 7.2.2. Three-Note Groupings 89
- 7.3 • Four-limb linear cycles workout 92

Session 8: Groove Construction 1: The Paradiddle Series Rudiments 93

    8.1• A List of Paradiddle Series on Snare Drum 94

    8.2• Passive linear groove adaptation 98

    8.3• Workouts for Passive Linear Groove Adaptation 101

Session 9: Hi-Hat Control 105

    9.1• Closed Hi-Hat 105

    9.2• Open Hi-Hat 106

    9.3• Open/Closed Hi-Hat 106

Session 10: Groove Construction 2: Dual Dynamic Layers Workout 111

    Instructions 111

    Figures 113

Session 11: Sonic Vocabulary and Chops Construction 123

    11.1• Sonic Vocabulary 123

    11.2• Case Study: Chops Analysis—Factorization 124

    11.3• Sonic Vocabulary Workout Routine 130

    11.4• Review 143

Conclusion 153

Index 155

Thank you, my parents, for your endless support and love.

Thank you Yaya for your company and assistance in making this book tangible. Without you, this book would have remained a bunch of random ideas.

Thank you Rob Carson for your mentorship, which unfolds the insight of the art of drumming.

Thank you Chuck Silverman, your spirit will always be carried on in my journey while exploring the art of drumming.

Thank you Matt Garstka, your mentorship and inspiration will always motivate me to break any mental and physical boundaries to go as far as I could in this journey of drumming.

Introduction

Teaching one to fish is better than giving one the fish.

This book is designed to present the linear applications over the drum-set from an analytical approach, so you won't be presented with some specific licks and groove transcriptions to memorize. Instead, the book itself offers an example of how to get into a particular playing style you would like to master. If you obtain the ability of generalization and summarization using an analytical approach, you could use them to break down any style of music you are interested in.

Presenting exact licks and transcriptions is like offering you fish, but showing the analytical approach is like teaching you how to fish. Knowing how to fish mainly indicates that if you have the tools and the environment, you would potentially have infinite fish. So don't look at those fish, but think more about how to fish.

The goal is to help you speak better via drums, and to eventually integrate this linear playing style into your repertoire in order to create something unique.

Part 1 of the book is the preparation phase containing sessions 1-3. These help you get into the mindset of establishing a good sound, learn how to use a metronome wisely, and examine the bass drum placement.

Part 2 is the constructing phase containing sessions 4-11. This part includes a practical example analysis that will show you how to use linear applications; as well as, the workout materials for linear coordination, sticking vocabularies, sonic vocabularies, linear groove, and linear chops.

Remember that physical training serves as a tool to better represent your mind. It is a workout routine to improve your mind-body connection.

Please visit:

http://www.langzhaomusic.com/book-a1

for video resources of the book.

Video resource libraries will be regularly updated with new materials to assist your learning process.

Your access code is: PA1B2016

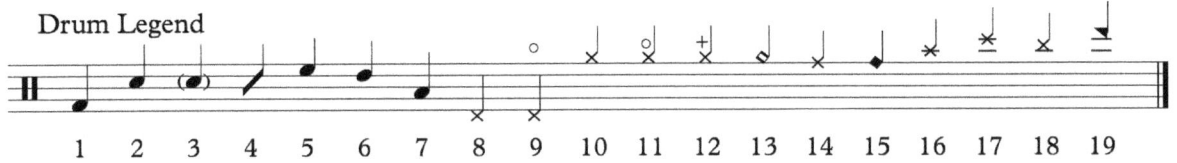

1. Kick	8. Hi-hat foot step	15. Ride bell
2. Snare	9. Hi-hat foot splash	16. Low crash
3. Snare ghost note	10. Hi-hat	17. High crash
4. Snare rim shot	11. Open Hi-hat start	18. Splash
5. High tom	12. Open Hi-hat end (Close)	19. Stack
6. Mid tom	13. Open Hi-hat	
7. Low tom	14. Ride	

PART 1
Preparations

Part 1 is the preparation phase that contains three sessions, in which we will discuss the following topics:

1. Tone and touch
2. Dynamic balance of each part of the drums
3. Creative uses of the metronome
   a. Micro approach for subdivision rate accuracy
   b. Macro approach for the general stabilization of time and feel
4. Bass drum placement diagnosis

While integrating the characteristics of gospel drumming into your grooves and chops, you've probably shared the same doubts as many others—it just doesn't sound right. Something is missing that sets apart your attempts from the gospel drummer. You could learn the licks and chops from your favorite gospel drummer verbatim, however, have you ever focused on the hidden side of the transcriptions?

The diverse languages of drumming share a similar root vocabulary that can be found within each style. For example, you can find a paradiddle in all genres of drumming, but it is how you apply a particular combination of touch, tone quality, phrasing, note placement and other key factors that dictate what genre this paradiddle belongs to. It is why we are focusing on the topics above, to first add the appropriate sound to your repertoire.

You will also examine and clean up your playing by going through the housekeeping stages before the intensive study on the linear applications in part 2.

With a solid foundation of consistency, accuracy on control and sound, you can just adapt the information in part 2 and enjoy all the effort that you put in during part 1.

SESSION 1

The Most Important Factor when Approaching a New Style of Music: Proper Sound

British drum master Simon Phillips once said that the drum sound you hear could be affected by the selection of different drums, microphones, etc. but that 90% of it was due to the way you play them. Of course, he talked in that thick British accent.

English has different accents. Music is just like languages; each genre has its sonic characteristics. Mastering a style of drumming is like learning that accent. If you can project that sound effectively, you already have one foot in the door. In this book, we are researching and adapting the sonic characteristic of gospel-influenced drumming, because it is indeed one of the most demanding sounds in the world of contemporary music.

- *Touch and Tone*

Looking at the drummers like Robert "Sput" Searight, Chris Coleman, Larnell Lewis, Gordon Campbell and many others, they all have exceptional control over the sound they create on the drums. At any dynamic level, these drummers' sound quality and intensity does not suffer.

Playing loud and powerful is necessary for different situations, such as to match the intensity of the songs, to drive the emotion to an individual level, and to cut through the choir and band while not being amplified a lot of times.

That tight, explosive, and cracking tonality with a compressed dynamic range is one of the characteristics gospel-influenced drummers have.

However, many drummers from a gospel drumming background are exposed to a great variety of styles of music. Different training paths and routines also give them many different touches over the drums. For example, you may find drummers like Robert "Sput" Searight, Chris "Daddy" Dave and Larnell Lewis also have a very elegant and smooth "jazz" touch with a broad range of dynamics. Again the key here is that at any dynamic level, these drummers' sound quality and intensity does not suffer.

- *Staccato and Definition*

Gospel drummers usually project a very *staccato* sound that gets in and out of the drums quickly. With a very *defined attack, a staccato* playing style also increases the *definition* of each note; it almost contains a bouncing motion that jumps out of the drums.

We have to increase the *velocity* at the moment of initiating a stroke, with a stronger *impulse* to create the sound we mentioned above. Please notice that generating this impulse is an instantaneous event. This stronger impulse you generate will add a stronger attack to the notes you play. It is important to keep in mind that adding velocity does not equal killing the rebound and pressing into the drums. Rebound does not only give the drum more breath and round out the tone you create, but it also helps your motion over the drums become more efficient. The goal is to get that full and staccato sound with increased definition. A brilliant resource you could use to significantly improve your control over rebound is George Stone's classic book "Accent and Rebound."

- *Consistency of Sound, Power and Endurance*

Even though sometimes it is not easy to maintain the consistency over the drums, the definition of each note should not suffer while being carried around the drums, regardless of the playing surfaces. Therefore, we have to improve the consistency of sound to limit the fluctuation of our produced sound, (at least in the style of music we are talking about throughout the book.)

Consistency over the drums requires a quick adjustment and adaptation to the change of rebound from different surfaces. It is also harder to keep that staccato texture of notes when playing them on bigger size floor toms than on the snare because the tension of the drumhead will offer a different feel and rebound. Follow the exercise below to check the consistency of your sound projection on various surfaces. Make sure you feel the rebound of various surfaces and adapt to them as quick as possible.

Remember that your sound quality and consistency should be maintained throughout any volume, speed, or any combination of both. Look for a staccato, full and round tone. Start slow, gradually increase speed to work on your endurance, while maintaining the sound quality we discussed above. In addition, work these passages at different volumes. Play with a metronome and mark the quarter note pulse with your hi-hat. Check how well you can maintain the consistency of the sound over different surfaces at different tempos.

Exe 1.1: Quick Endurance Workout

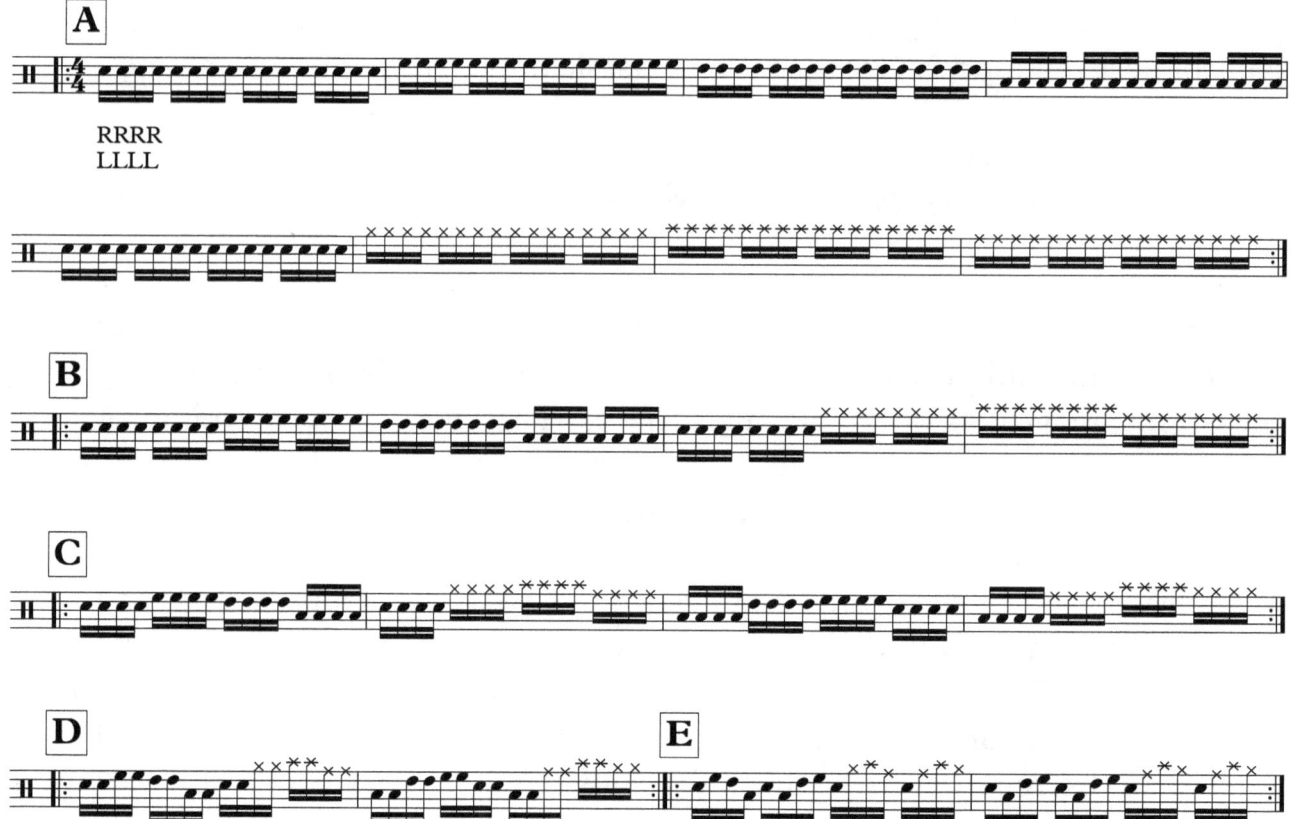

- *Weight Distribution of Key Voices*

Weight distribution between key voices is affected by the genres of music you play. The combination of the kick, hat and the snare form the center voices of what's happening in the grooves of gospel, RnB, and Hip-Hop drumming. Grooves and pockets are built from the bottom up; from the bass drum to the snare then to the cymbals as opposed to Jazz, which is built top down from the ride, to the snare and on to the bass drum. The weight of the grooves and pockets should always gravitate towards the bass drum in these examples. This concept also applies to other contemporary genres such as rock, pop, funk, etc.

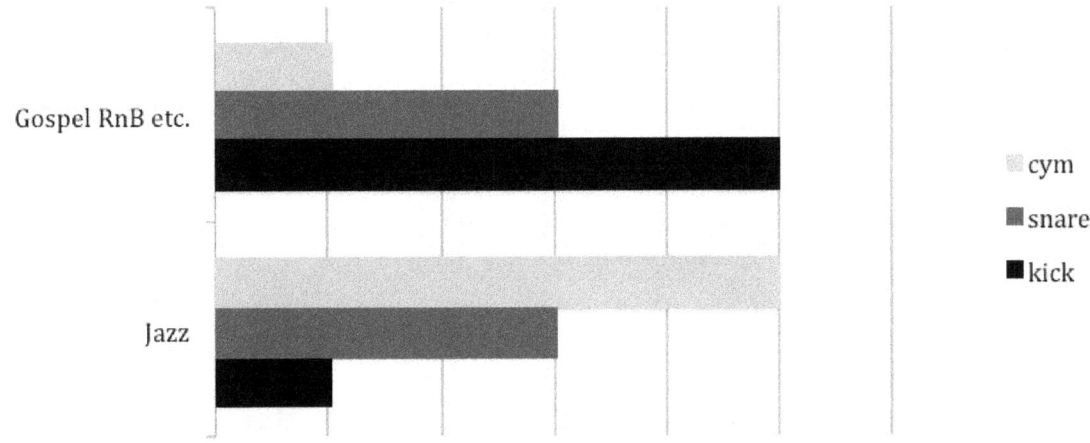

Weight Distribution of the Voices

- *Dynamic balance among the key voices*

Since we have a bottom-up structure of the weight distribution to the key voices, the internal dynamic among these voices should be balanced correspondingly. Having the voices unbalanced will lead to an entirely different feel of the groove or pocket you create.

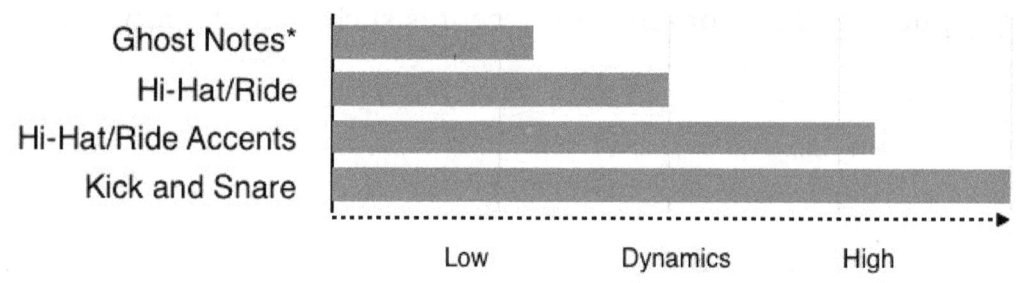

*Ghost note control is not covered in this book. We will discuss that in the upcoming technique book.

- *Gears*

It is tricky to say what drums and cymbals you should use. A jazz bop kit with high tuning will definitely not work, and a big rock kit with open tuning may not function either. Generally, under the gospel content, snare drums are tuned fairly tight to project a cracking sound, toms sing well with a round and full tone, while the bass drums are tuned deep and solid.

Cymbal wise, it is more of a personal taste and it usually varies among different situations that are shaped by both musical content and style. Again, gospel-influenced drummers are becoming the dominant force in many genres. The artists or projects want the sound, energy, phrasing, etc. these drummers can generate.

However, the choice of gear should fit the style. It is important to work on the style of music within its defining sound, which is the foundation of developing a good feel. What we discussed above covers two aspects of the authenticity of sound—the sound the instruments project and the sound you generate. The latter one is always more important, as it will help you to manipulate and shape the sounds, rather than relying too much on the gear you use.

- *About the Linear Playing Style*

Linear drumming creates a different flow to your grooves and chops compared to ostinato based drumming. However, it requires a different type of balance and coordination of your limbs. In this book, we will look into how to build linear coordination and construct grooves first. Afterwards, we will create improvisational chops from the grooves, in order to maximize musicality and make better statements over the drums.

SESSION 2

Training on Timing and Note Placement Accuracy: The Metronome

The metronome is used every day by musicians to improve timing. However, by manipulating the metronome in different ways, the process of time improvement could be done in a more effective and efficient way. Let's talk about how to use metronome creatively to improve your timing and note placement accuracy.

2.1 • NOTE PLACEMENT:

Visualizing Your Note Placement

Visually, if you recorded yourself into any DAW, the grid you set up in the session represents the pulse and the referencing subdivision on your choice. If you are on top of the beat, your waveforms of corresponding subdivision should fall right on top of that grid line. Accordingly, playing ahead and behind the beat should be visually represented by waveforms falling slightly before or after the grid line.

Example of a 16th note grid, note is on top of the grid line.

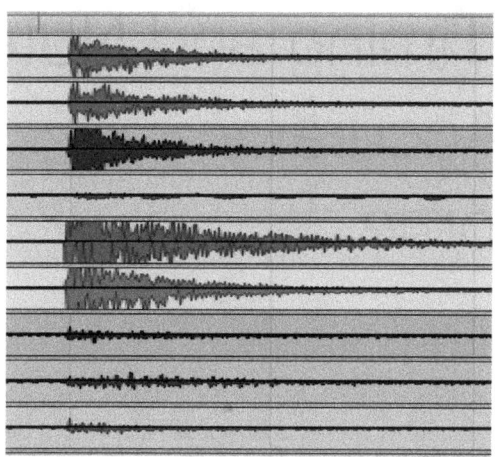

Hearing Your Note Placement

To hear your note placement, try to compare the attack of the metronome click to your note. When playing on top of the beat, you should be able to cancel the metronome click, because the attack of your metronome click is aligned and masked by your note. Correspondingly, playing ahead and behind the click should generate a subtle gap between your note and the click. Make sure that your metronome is set at a proper volume so that you are not getting a false cancellation of the attack.

Feeling Your Note Placement

Where to place each note can be a personal choice. A lot of the times it is all about how you feel and what the music needs. Playing before the beat offers a little more driving feel energy wise, while playing behind the beat gives the music a relaxed feel. Different music may require different placements. Even within a song, various parts may need different note placements. It is important to maintain that subtlety of placement in accordance to the pulse, so that it keeps a stable flow within a comfortable range for the listener. The feel for note placement can be recognized/developed within a practical situation. How you and your bandmates place the note compared to each other will dictate your overall feel. For example, if the guitarist is playing slightly ahead of you, you don't have to play behind your pulse to create a laid back feel.

2.2 • CONSISTENCY AND MICRO- APPROACH—

To force you to pay attention to each subdivision

The consistency of how well you manage the space between each note will affect the stability of flow and your larger scope of timing. If in a 4/4-meter with a 16th note based groove, your distance between each 16th notes varies, the length of each quarter note value will vary as well; resulting in an unstable groove. Using a metronome to regulate consistency could be done in the following ways: (All examples refer to a 4/4-meter, 16th note based groove.)

Marking all Subdivisions (Passive Correction following the Reference)

Set your metronome to mark all the subdivisions, for example, in a 4/4-16th note based groove, set your metronome to mark each 16th note. Align each of the notes you play to the corresponding subdivision marked by the metronome. Make sure you pay attention to the attack of the note you are playing, as well as the attack of the click. Start very slow to check the relationship between the notes you are playing and the subdivisions the metronome is marking. Maintain that relationship and gradually increase the speed you are practicing.

In this situation, your mind is passively following the reference, getting feedback, and then making corrections to adjust any notes that are misplaced.

Example.2.2.1

Marking the Es and As (Active Adjustment)

Marking the Es and As is a more advanced way to work on the subdivision note placement accuracy. In this case, what you reference (the click) is permutated against your groove. When the click is permutated to mark the Es and As, you don't hear the downbeat in the reference anymore. Your mind is forced to actively spot all of the subdivisions instead of having them marked out by the metronome, where you are passively following a reference.

When only hearing Es and As from the click, you are made to internalize and maintain the space between each subdivision actively. If the clicks start to shuffle rather than aligning with your notes, it reflects the shifting of your accuracy of note placement.

Quick tip: *How fast you can play is a matter of how fast you can hear the subdivisions of Es and As; how fast you can hear is dependent on how fast your mind can process these offbeat subdivisions.*

Example 2.2.2

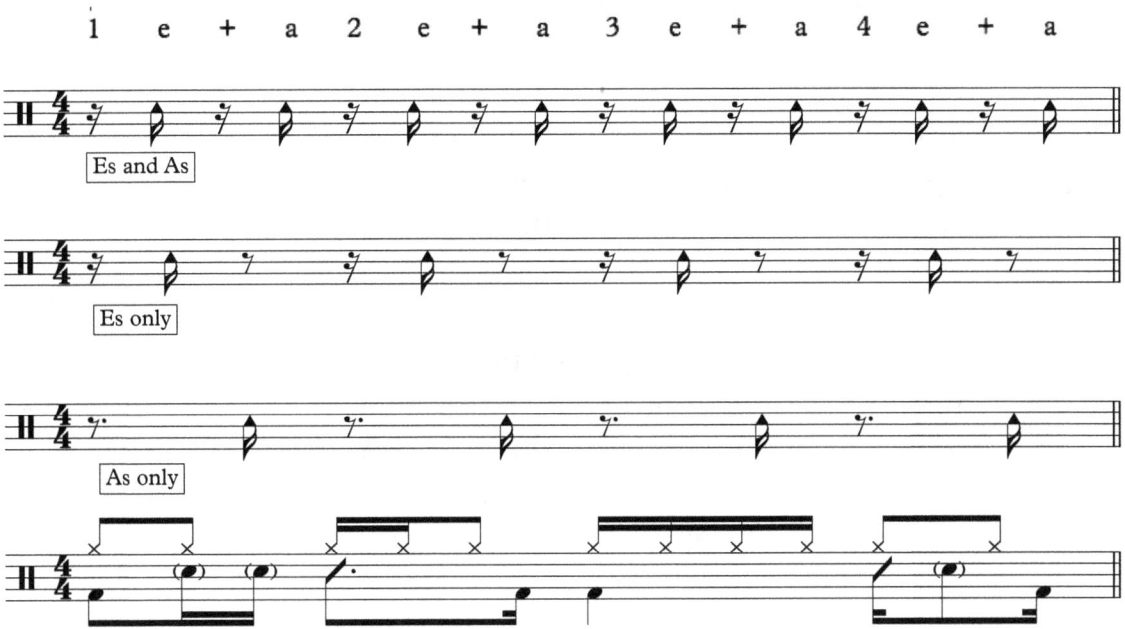

2.3 • TIME FEEL STABILITY AND MACRO-APPROACH:

Back to the Pulse

Although referencing your playing to the metronome on a subdivision based micro-approach is an excellent way to improve your sense on the consistency of note placement, you will have to come back to the quarter note pulse (we are still using 4/4 as examples).

You have to come back to the larger scope of the groove to make it feel good. Placing every note at the right spot is only one aspect of timing, and you should never forget the feel. A good example of this was taught to me when I studied with Will Kennedy from the Yellowjackets. He pointed out to me the different ways you could reference your metronome with a Funk/Songo groove.

Example 2.3.1

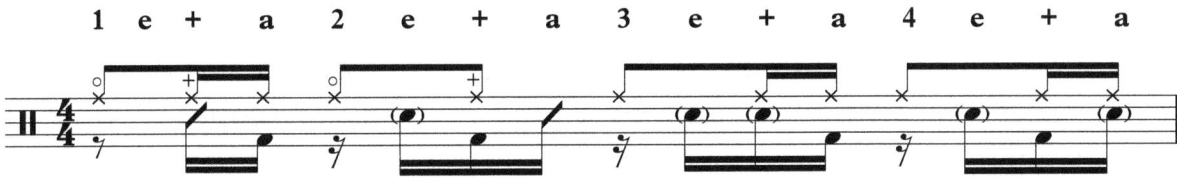

If you are referencing all subdivisions when playing this groove, the balance of the groove tends to spread evenly to each subdivision; doing this usually means that there will be less of a chance of gravitating towards the quarter note, which tends to make the feel suffer.

A Songo pattern in any situation is always accenting the Es and As itself, leaving the quarter note pulse on a weak voice (hi-hat). Therefore, the pulse is more implied rather than played. In this situation, your mind has to be set at the quarter note pulse, so as to gravitate the subdivisions around it; energy wise it is not going to be an even spread among the 16th notes. Rather, it will have peaks appearing around the pulse, to make this groove sit in a position that feels right.

> *Focusing on the accuracy of each subdivision will clean up your playing, and focusing on the actual pulse of the groove will let you gain a better feel. Remember these two approaches are not conflicting each other, but complementing each other.*

Larger Pulses and Internal Clock

Once you gain control of playing from the micro approach and develop a feel from the macro approach, we can move on to even bigger scopes of your time, feel, and stability.

For example, setting your metronome for whole notes and marking only each bar. Now you are primarily maintaining everything with your internal clock because the metronome reference has become more or less just a checkpoint. Theoretically, if you control your variables to have a consistent flow of rate, time, feel and tone quality, you should be able to maintain good timing on a larger scope. However, as human beings we are distracted by so many other factors, so working on your internal clock with larger pulses is always a good option to follow up your micro and macro training on timing.

To put all in a nutshell, we have discussed how to develop a good time and feel creatively by using the metronome as a reference. In the next session, we will have a series of exercises to facilitate your understanding of the process we discussed above.

SESSION 3

Base Drum Placements

For all the exercises in this session, please focus first on your sound as discussed in the previous session. Make sure that you have a good velocity when you generate your strokes to create that staccato sound. Follow the metronome system for each of the exercises. Start slow to check your note placement, then gradually work your speed up. These are the foundation exercises for the upcoming sessions. In this session, we will work on note placement, consistency, endurance, timing, basic 4-way coordination, and the internalization of subdivisions.

Recording your practice is recommended; do not go to the next metronome system or exercise until you gain full control of the current one. The objective is to be able to execute without breaks and mistakes for more than 2 minutes during each take. Make sure you count out loud. All the materials should be worked both straight and swung, if you have extra time, please work on both open hand and close hand positions; this will open up some new possibilities for your phrasing.

3.1• COUNTING SYSTEM:

Counting out loud not only tracks your playing, but it also adds some natural organic flow and feel to your playing by forcing you to breathe. Learn to breathe while playing will influence your phrasing organically. Think about how horn players phrase their playing. Drummers sometimes could be too busy since we don't have to blow our notes out. In addition, many drummers have a tendency to hold their breath until the completion of tricky passages where the physical requirement is high. When you start to count, you will naturally start to breathe and feel more relaxed while you play, which will in turn will give you a better timing consistency and feel. Counting is like adding an extra limb on top of your 4-way coordination that helps you gain more control for you playing.

- *Straight Counting*

You can manipulate to count any combinations. For example, on an 8th note based counting it would be "1+2+3+4+", or on a quarter note pulse based counting it could simply be "1 2 3 4".

An Analytical Approach to Linear Applications | 31

- *Swung Counting*

It is very common to swing in a gospel, RnB and Hip-Hop based situation, so the counting for swung would be:

At a slower tempo, you could count out all subdivisions to place the notes at their correct place. When you increase the speed, simplify the counting by leaving out the middle triplet. (Shown in the example above.)

3.2 • METRONOME SYSTEM:

The following metronome system should be applied throughout the exercises in the whole book. You should be able to internalize the Es and As very effectively after you work through all the exercises.

- *Microscope References*

- *Macroscope References*

You could swing the metronome clicks in the same way to mark the swung subdivision. However, make sure that you check back with the feel of the swung passage because a lot of times the notes are not placed "dead on" their position; the third triplet note sometimes is pushed back a little bit just to provide an even harder swing feel.

3.3 • Bass Drum Placement, Hi-Hat Foot Control, and Basic 4-way Coordination:

In this exercise, both your hands will be playing all 16th note subdivisions, while your right-hand marks the quarter note pulse as accents on the bell of the ride, and your left-hand marks the back beat of 2 and 4 with a rimshot. All other subdivisions should be ghost notes. Make sure that you remember the dynamic distribution we talked about in previous discussions. Your hi-hat foot will be marking time under 8th note subdivisions by splashing and closing the hi-hat. Make sure your note placement aligns with the ones played by each limb. Go through the entire placement alignment exercises under your selected metronome system from A to D. Make sure that you count out loud.

EX 3.3.1: bass drum placement and endurance workout

An Analytical Approach to Linear Applications | 35

C Three-note permutation

D Unison workout

EX 3.3.2: Bass drum melodies one to four-note

EX 3.3.3: Bass Drum Melodies Odd Grouping Phrases and Over-the-Barline

In the following exercises, the bass drum melody is phrased with odd groupings of 3, 5 and 7. This makes the phrases resolve over the barline, which as you will notice, means that not all of them start at the down beat. Make sure you count out loud, so your bass drum phrasing is actually playing to your internal clock. Gradually get used to the feeling and remember the flow of these odd groupings against 4/4 meters.

Bass drum placement is vital, because in the Gospel, RnB, HipHop, Funk, etc. genres, the grooves are built bottom-up from the bass drum as we talked about in previous sessions. All the exercises above are an excellent way to adjust and align your physical balance, dynamic balance, note placement, consistency, timing and most importantly your awareness of flaws. You are not only training your hands and feet to be more accurate, but also training your mind and ears to be able to pick up more precise timing. Playing drums is advanced multitasking.

PART 2
Practical Applications of Grooves and Chops

Again, it is important to remember that different styles of drumming share a lot of common vocabularies, and the difference of sound and time-feel is what makes them different and unique. In part 1, we have discussed some of the key sonic and time-feel characteristics so that we can establish a good hearing foundation that would facilitate the subsequent practical application studies. In part 2, we will hit the following topic to start to build up the mind-body connection on linear drumming under the gospel content.

1. Linear Applications

    a. Linear Groove
    b. Linear Chops

2. Sonic Vocabularies

    a. Sonic Patterns
    b. Sticking Possibilities
    c. Rudimental Analysis
    d. Orchestration

3. Establishing Musical Phrases with Sonic Vocabularies

4. Constructing Chops Consciously

The object is to find out how ideas are formed, not just to learn them superficially as it appears to be. We will start by analyzing an example demonstrated by Henry McDaniel IV that perfectly represents the use of linear applications under the gospel content. After that, we will go through a series of systematic training on both the technical and mindset aspects to help you achieve the level of performance in the demonstration video.

SESSION 4

Linear Applications and Demo Analysis

Linear drumming is a general mono-layer voice approach. For the most part, there is a single voice flow, which occasionally has more than one voice appearing in unison. Much like a monophonic instrument which generates single line melodies while implying the harmonies, linear drumming suggests the effort of what an ostinato based application could offer, but with a different interpretation of the flow and feel. Drummers like David Garibaldi and Steve Gadd are considered as having added significant influences to this style of drumming.

Please take a look at the Songo influenced groove examples below. Both grooves share the same key voices but are structured differently in two fashions:

Linear vs. Ostinato based Application

Linear Groove Application: Single Voicing

Non-Linear Ostinato Groove Application: Multiple Voicing

An Analytical Approach to Linear Applications

Here are some general thoughts on how linear applications are different than the ostinato based applications.

	Ostinato-based Applications	**Linear Applications**
Voices	Polyphonic	Monophonic (Most of the time)
Coordination Development	Ostinato voices could function as reference for counter-parts Independence among parallel voices Interdependence in the same voices	All limb interdependence for the single voice
Rate	Some layers of voices may restrict the rate of flow due to the difficulty of executing at certain speed	Contains more alternate motions among limbs, more useful at higher rate of flow
Flow	Ostinato may create independence challenges, but it also helps to regulate the accuracy of the counter-voices Implied note-to-note flow, borrowing notes from other voices.	Accuracy of rate of flow becomes more difficult and needs stronger interdependence between limbs Note-to-note flow, higher intensity

4.1 • DEMO:

Please go over the drum interpretation by Henry McDaniel IV for the jam track "Drive It" by Kaz Rodriguez. This interpretation is an excellent example of constructing linear applications, both on the grooves and chops. I have provided a note-by-note transcription as a reference for the insight of Henry's performance. Please keep in mind that a transcription is a tool for the analysis of how and why to use these linear applications, the goal is not for you to play that transcription in order to feel accomplished, but to understand the logic behind it and be able to craft your interpretation efficiently.

The analysis will be focusing on the construction of grooves, fills, and longer passages of chops in a linear fashion. When you hear the key aspects of the music, you should be aiming to reflect that in your playing. The importance of this is to make your drumming correspond with techniques and vocabulary that fit the music. It is critical to know why something is performed in a certain way, be conscious of your action and establish a strong mind-body connection, which will make in your statement on the drums a more meaningful one.

DRIVE IT

Music by Kaz Rodriguez
Drums interpreted by Henry McDanel IV
As transcribed by Lang Zhao

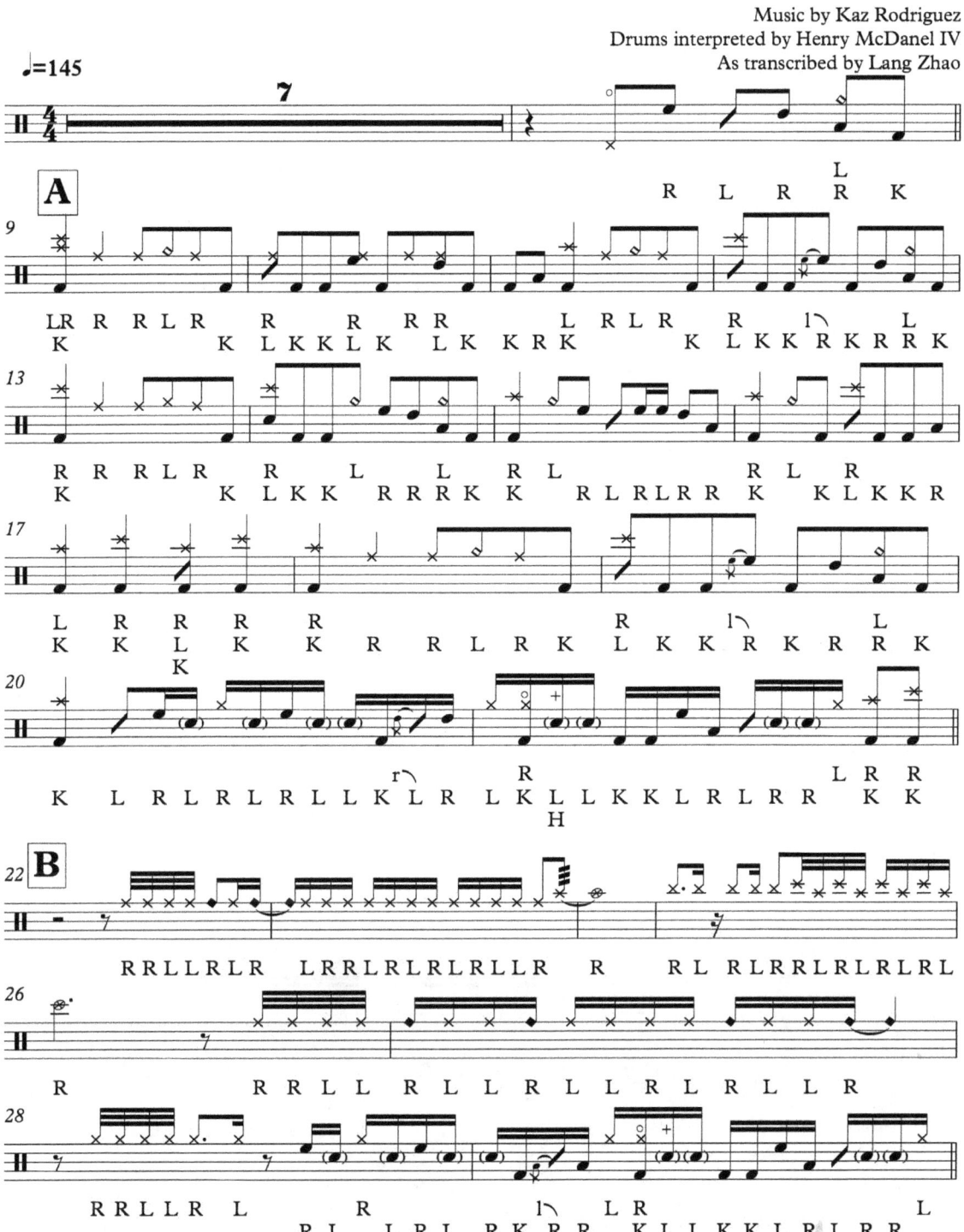

An Analytical Approach to Linear Applications | 47

48 | *Lang Zhao*

As you went through the track, you should have been able to tell that the entire song is 16th note subdivision based. At 145 bpm, the flow is steady but has a driving kind of feel to it.

Most of the interpretation uses linear concepts, including grooves, fills, and longer passages of chops. The applied half-time feel also allows the entire groove to better sit on top of the fast pace of the 16th note flow at 145 bpm. A linear concept ideally generates the intensity of the note-to-note flow, which on the other hand would be hard to achieve via an ostinato-based application at this tempo.

4.2 • Groove Construction:

All the grooves below are straight out of Henry's interpretation. The structures of the grooves are all focused around the kick variations and snare backbeat on 3. Everything else is an implemented softer dynamic layer in the same linear voice generated between the hi-hat and snare drum ghost notes. This should be a principle of creating a linear based groove: settle on a kick and snare skeleton and then figure out a connection between notes. It is critical to keep a clear dynamic difference between the skeleton and the filled-up notes. Implying the dynamic layer inside the linear flow is important. Otherwise, the groove would fail.

52 | *Lang Zhao*

Section B1 (00:01:05)

The groove above is the first half-time 16th note based groove that appears in the interpretation. In measure 30, the first note is doubled with a crash as a statement of the beginning of the groove. In linear applications, you may occasionally see double or triple voices used at a highlight point.

4.2.1 Define the Skeleton and the Subdivision of Flow

The skeleton of the groove is a two bar phrase.

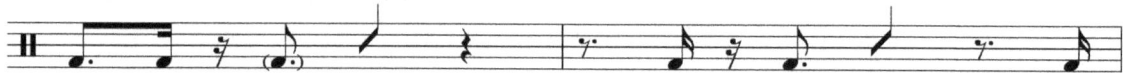

In order to catch the 16th note subdivision flow in the track, a note-to-note 16th note embellishment is to be added around the skeleton to fill up the holes.

4.2.2 Define a Skeleton

There are many options to fill up the spaces here, for example, using toms to create a melodic line, or as Henry did here, using a tightly closed hi-hat sound and snare drum ghost notes. Make note of the difference between the embellishment and the skeleton sonic wise. The object is to keep the groove's flow by

An Analytical Approach to Linear Applications | 53

maintaining the skeleton. An embellishment should never weaken the skeleton. Tom melodies are a heavier sounding approach when the music calls for that dynamically. The hi-hat and snare ghost note embellishment, however, differ from the skeleton in dynamics and sound texture. The tight and crispy closed hi-hat sound has a similar sonic quality to the snare ghost notes when playing at a low volume, which implies a legato feel to the groove and makes the skeleton stand out.

4.2.3 Sonic Vocabulary Elements

Sonic vocabularies are a broader concept compared to sticking vocabularies; they are a pattern of sound that you hear. It could come from a melody or a rhythm you hear in the musical content, or simply from your own creation. All sticking vocabularies contain a corresponding motion that creates a sonic pattern orchestrated with different voices. If we take the sonic patterns of the sticking only and apply stickings to achieve the same sonic goal, it does not necessarily require the same sticking pattern. Sticking is a sufficient but not necessary condition to sonic results. Sticking vocabulary is the tool used to help you interpret the ideas you hear, and it is as or even more important as anything else to be able to hear more sonic vocabulary because that's where everything starts.

In groove B1, the vocabularies can be put into two major elements as marked in different colors.

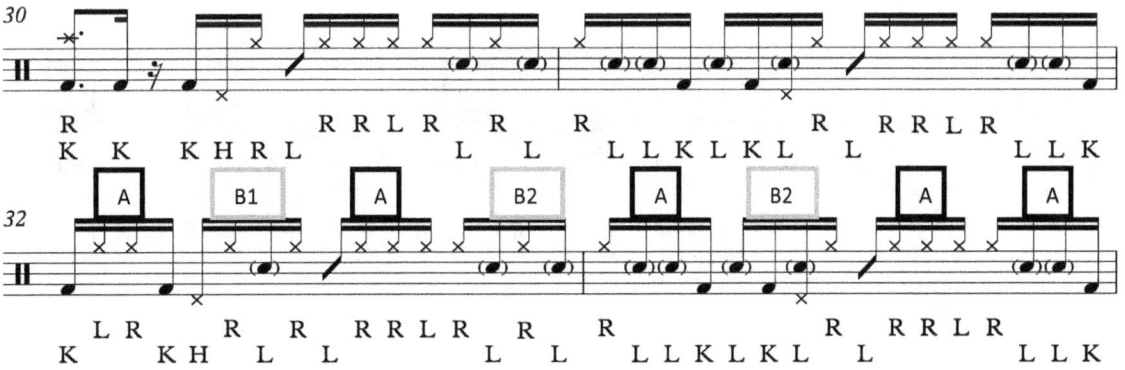

A type of 4-note patterns are structured from the sonic characteristic of inverted paradiddles:

R L L R   L R R L

1. The middle two notes carry identical sonic quality due to the double sticking.

2. The first note of each 4-note grouping comes from an alternative sticking R to L or L to R. There is always a new cycle of motion flow that starts at the first note, so there is an implied accent

3. The last note ends the cycle and prepares the new cycle.

Because of these reasons, we could say that the key sonic characteristic of the inverted paradiddle is found in the identical middle notes, and the first note and last note can be orchestrated any way upon need. Thus in groove B1 we can put all the 4-note groupings that contain identical middle notes together and mark them as type A patterns.

?   ?

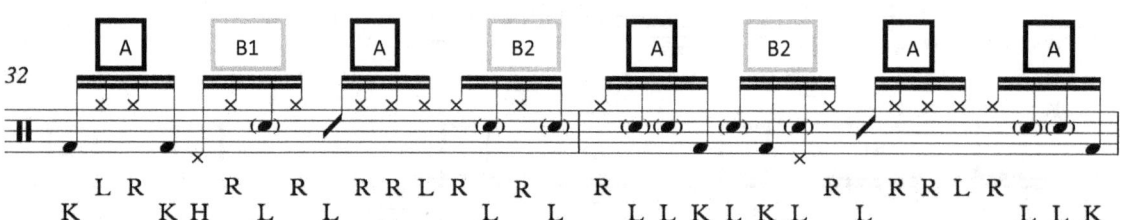

The Same analytical procedure can be applied to B patterns as well. B patterns are based on alternative singles sticking in two ways:

Sonic pattern B1 remains the second and fourth note of the 4-note grouping with the same sound source, while other notes are orchestrated on different sound sources. B2 is the opposite of B1. The first B1 pattern altered the hand stroke to a step-closed hi-hat, but it will not change the sonic characteristic of the alternated singles orchestrated around the drums.

Now let's take a look at the C-section of the song.

Section C (00:01:18)

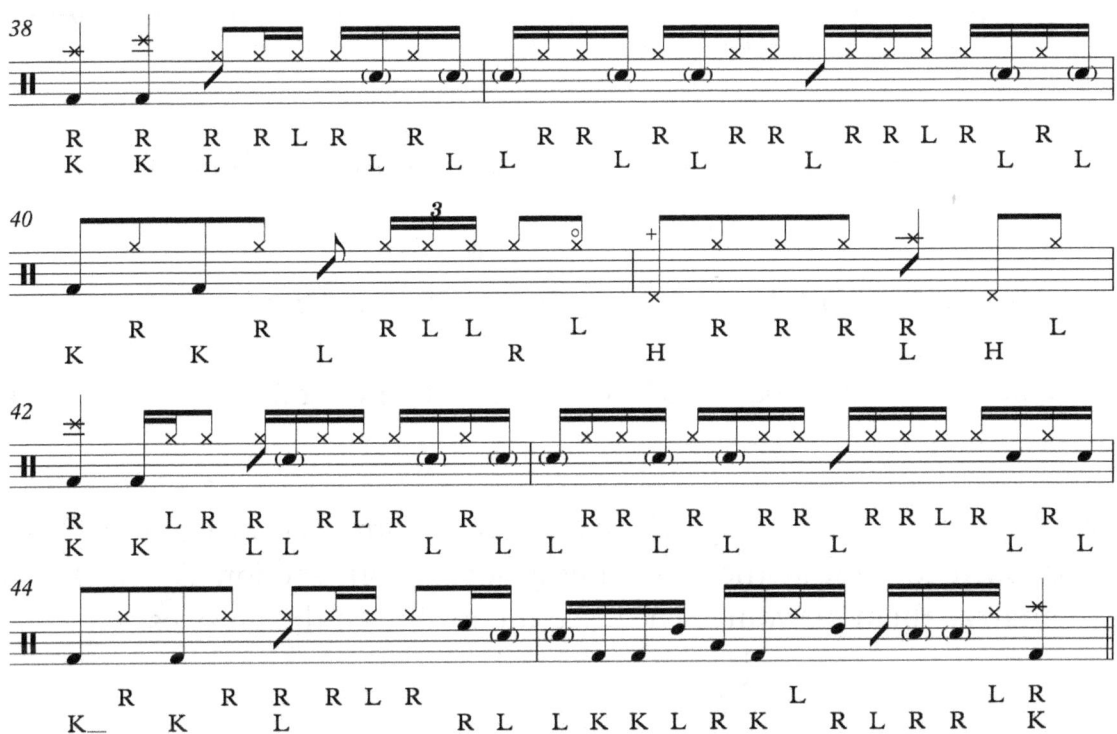

Let's use the same steps to look at this section.

Section C contains two 4-bar phrases, in which the figure from the music is

Accordingly, the groove's skeleton is laid out as:

where on beat 3 of the last bar is accented with a crash to catch the figure.

The first two bars of section C carry over the elements of the B section using identical linear ideas except for adding in a paradiddle vocabulary.

This 16-bar phrase consists of two 8-bar phrases in the following structure:

| 16th note based | 16th note based | 8th note based | 8th note based |

| 16th note based | 16th note based | 8th note based | 16th note fill setting up for beat 4 |

As we have previously analyzed, the grooves from section B1 and C use the same approach to look at the following grooves from section D and E. See if you can analyze them on your own to see the insight of the grooves.

An Analytical Approach to Linear Applications | 57

Exercise 1: Linear Groove Construction Analysis

Section D (00:01:45)

Section E (00:02:11)

Questions:

1. What should be captured in the musical content?

2. What is the groove's skeleton? How does it relate to the musical content?

3. How is the skeleton embellished? In what sonic theme? How is the embellishment supporting the skeleton?

4. What is the sonic vocabulary used? What rudiment/sticking could achieve such sonic characteristic? How did the orchestration evolve from the rudiment/sticking?

58 | Lang Zhao

4.3 • CHOPS CONSTRUCTION:

Fills and chops are embellishments to the musical content. Good execution will let the music shine. Otherwise, they could only ruin the moment. In this interpretation, we can find the use of chops in 3 clear stages:

1. As fills transitioning to figures or new sections
2. Inside of the grooves under the musical content
3. Long passages of chops as free improvisation under the musical content

The execution of chops in the interpretation is never unconscious. As we analyze through the following passages, we will not only see how linear applications are very useful in building chops, but also how chops are oriented around the elements of the groove, musical content, as well as how to go beyond the content.

4.3.1 CHOPS AS FILLS

Let's look at bar 44-45 in section C, where the setup for a figure happens:

Section C (00:01:18)

The groove's skeleton is maintained here (as analyzed previously in the groove construction section) while the fill happens to setup the figure on beat 4 in bar 45. It is a very practical approach to keeping the backbeat in the fill, which maintains the flow of groove and makes the fill blend in more seamlessly. The fill itself started on the "+" of beat 4 in bar 44 and lasted until beat 4 at the end of the phrase.

The sonic vocabulary in this fill could be broken up into two parts, the implied melody is:

The first brackets marked out a 6-note grouping starting at the "+" of beat 4; two 16th note ghost notes are naturally added in the space to embellish this melody.

R L L K K L

The sonic vocabulary is identical to a left lead paradiddle-diddle displaced one 16th note ahead as shown below...

R L L K K L   R L L R R L   L R L L R R

This adds a closed hi-hat sound that glues the melody together and leads to the figure on beat 4 is marked out in the second bracket.

4.3.2. Chops Inside of the Grooves under the Musical Content

Section C1 (00:01:31)

Section C1 contains the same musical content. However, the interpretation is busier and acts as a build up for what happens in section C, which establishes the groove for the section. This section is an excellent example of chops inside of the groove under the musical content.

Here is the groove's skeleton from section C and C1 again:

An Analytical Approach to Linear Applications | 61

The interpretation in section C1 blends more chops into the groove and omits some repetitions of the skeleton. However, the skeleton remains the fundamental component as shown below. The slashes represent interpreted chops.

The sonic vocabularies from the passage basically could be put into the following categories:

This type of pattern (A) has the inverted paradiddle sonic quality.

The following diagram shows how the general sonic pattern is orchestrated in the groove

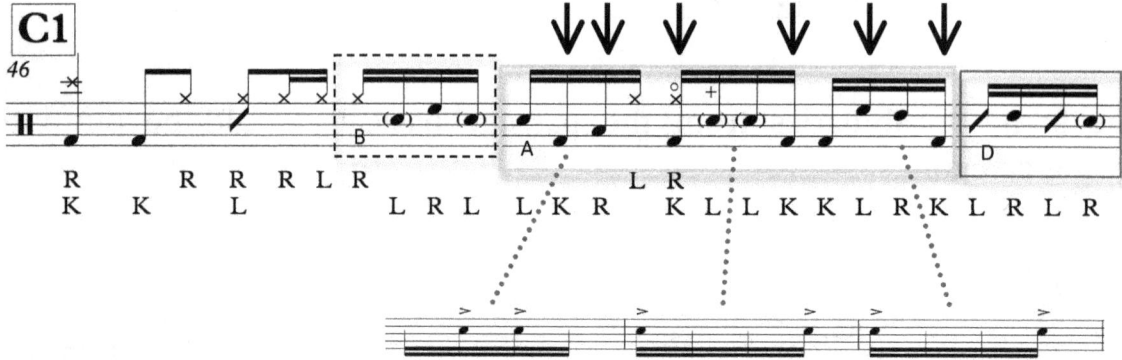

Note that in the first 4-note grouping of the (A) pattern; the snare ghost note on "1" and closed hi-hat on "1a" share similar sonic quality. We can think of them as the same source. The kick and floor tom on "1e" and "1+" are perceived as a stronger dynamic layer, making them stand out from the group. Therefore, we can place them under the following sonic pattern:

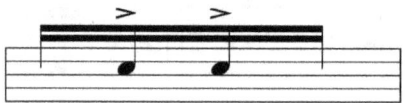

In the third 4-note grouping, the kick outlines the structure already, being placed on "3" and "3a", while the toms on "3e" and "3+" imply a different melody rather than a dynamic layer like the first 4-note grouping. We have addressed the two linear embellishments (melodic and dynamic) of the groove's skeletons in the prior section, and this applies to chops as well.

The next (A) pattern in the second line could be addressed in the following manner:

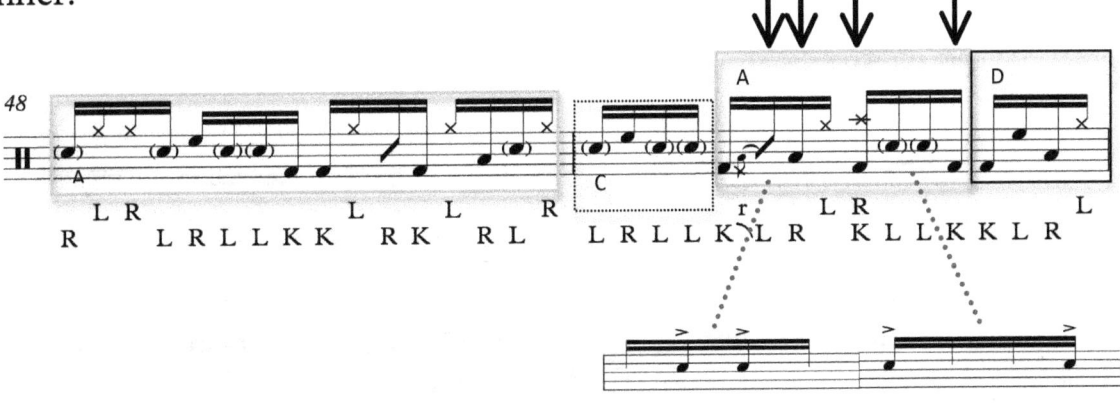

These 4 note groupings are on beat 3 and 4 in measure 49. On "3e" the snare rimshot is flammed with a floor tom accent, and then followed by "3+" as another floor tom hit. That's why sonically, it is perceived as pattern:

Type B is simply an alternating sonic pattern:

Type C includes some sonic patterns like the following:

Type D includes the following sonic patterns:

64 | *Lang Zhao*

4.3.3 Chops as Long Passages of Improvisation

Section G, G1 (00:02:59)

The ending sections, G and G1, are long passages of chops that are improvised using similar sonic vocabularies but with more intensive syncopation melodies. These sections are constructed by going out of the groove's skeleton yet remaining in the similar sonic vocabularies as discussed before. The intensity is higher than any section before it, so the energy is built up to push the ending of the song to the climax.

Section G starts with syncopated rhythms and some space, and is followed by busier orchestration around the toms. G1, the last 8 bar phrase, began with a metric modulation to regroup the 16th notes to 6-note groups. This phrase went over the bar-line to create a more rhythmic dissonance and resolves back to the 4-note groupings after. The last four bars are built up even more with the orchestration between snare rim shots and bass drum with crash hits on "e"s and "a"s. This creates even more rhythmic dissonance and finally resolves to a solid statement of descending tom rolls that mark the ending of the tune.

The entire energy contour of the interpretation can be marked out like the following graph:

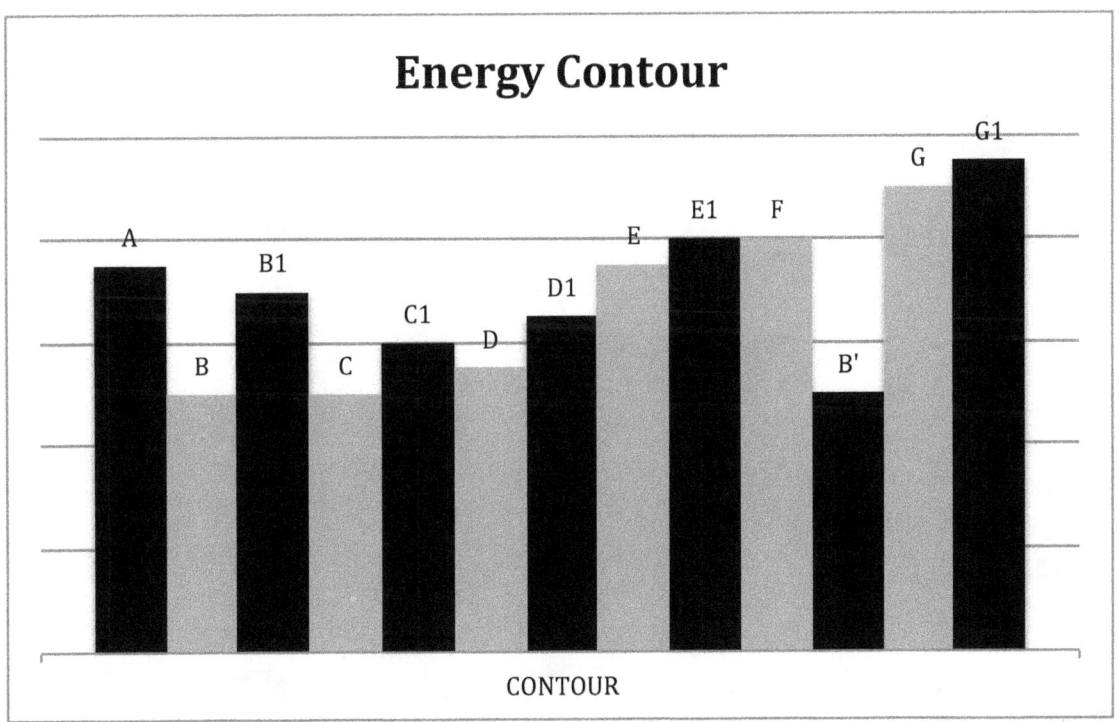

As you could see here, passages of chops are wisely used to outline this energy contour, which dynamically brings the track to life. It is critical to understand why chops are used here and how chops are executed. In this interpretation, chops are constructed on top of the grooves and being gradually expanded to create the energy contour of the track. Section A, B1, C, D E are majorly grooves with transitional fills to the next section. C1, D1, E1 as variations to the previous sections contain more chops build inside of the groove and creates that higher energy level. Sections B and B' are two lighter parts playing more on cymbals to prepare the flow of the upcoming sections. F is a shorter recap of the opening A section. G and G1 are the climaxes of the entire track that leads to the end of the tune, and these sections contain the longest passages of improvised chops.

An Analytical Approach to Linear Applications | 67

Exercise 2: Linear Chops Construction Analysis

Section G (00:02:59)

1. What are the most commonly used sonic vocabularies in this passage?
2. How are they related to the construction of the previous groove?
3. Outline the syncopated melodic rhythms among snare rimshots, kicks, and toms.

The analysis in this session breaks down Henry's interpretation. We looked at how the groove's skeleton is initiated accordingly to the music, and how the embellishments are added around the skeleton. We also looked at how the sonic vocabulary is used during the construction of grooves and chops. Notice how the chops and grooves are balanced throughout the music, which creates an energy contour.

The next sessions will look into the more technical side of linear applications; such as sticking patterns, coordination, and workouts to achieve a better mind-body connection on linear playing.

SESSION 5

A Word on Practice

As musicians, what we translate the ideas we have in our minds into physical actions. The ideal situation is to convert 100% of what we think into what we play, but there are always some mental and physical disruptions that occur during the translation process; it could be a physical boundary needs to break, or simply just a lack of mental preparation. In order to eliminate these factors, we practice. This term is probably the most used word in our daily life as musicians; but have you ever sat down and thought about what the term practice means?

Practice is explained in many references as a mastering of a particular goal by doing it over and over again. Every one of us has gone through this process more or less, but how come there are different results from different individuals? There might not be a universal answer that fits each person's situation, but there are many tools that you could use to inspire your way of creating a more efficient practice.

1. Repetition creates muscle memory - make sure that every repetition is what you intend to achieve. Bad habits are hard to correct.

2. Think about practicing slow differently - imagine doing observations under a time microscope that slows time down. Our brain processes unfamiliar information slowly. Slowing down gives your mind more time to react to the details of your actions; so building muscle memory is not only enhancing your physical muscle memory but also your mental muscle memory, which eventually will lead to a tighter mind-body connection.

3. Think about practicing fast differently – once you have stabilized your playing from practicing slow, it is very necessary to push and challenge your physical and mental ability to the edge gradually. This is the only way to break out of your physical and mental limitations. A sword will never get sharp if you don't sharpen the blade.

4. Always think about the mind-body connection – imagine that you connect your mind and body via broadband. Practice increases the bandwidth, which increases the speed of information exchange between your mind and body.

5. Memorize the feel when you are playing your instrument effectively – auditory perception could change depending on the acoustic environment. However, if you know what feels right when playing something, you are relying less on the factors you can't control and gaining more confidence and trust in yourself.

6. Concentration is mind training – the deeper you concentrate, the more efficient your practice will be. Concentration creates a better environment for improving your mind-body connection. The more you concentrate during practice, the better you could potentially maintain that concentration in practical situations.

7. Work on your hand rudiments with a metronome and always start slow – this will help you to establish a consistency of the rate of flow and make the accuracy of the subdivision placement over the drum set easier.

8. Focus on sound, touch, and note placements – these are the key factors that define an individual style. Fundamental techniques are universally adopted in all different styles, but it is the key factors that dictate how techniques should be modified for a particular style. Use your ears well.

9. 2-minute is an important length – you need to be able to execute the goal material repetitively for longer than 2 minutes without any flaws before you can say you have mastered it.

10. Know the importance of breaking the flow – after you have mastered certain material by repetition, make sure you break the flow and see if you can come back to it smoothly.

11. Make sure you do not play faster than you can think – always be conscious of what you speak via the drums.

12. Create a practice routine – it is an attitude toward life as well.

13. Study phrasing well – music is a language.

14. You are always as good as your worst day, so the less you suck on your worst day; the better you are on an entire level—Matt Garstka

Now let's get into the exercises in the upcoming sessions.

SESSION 6

Linear Coordination Part 1: Double-Note Interdependence

The following exercises are element patterns designed to enhance the relationship among the limbs. These elements could turn into many other combinations and patterns. Make sure to use a metronome as we discussed in Part 1. Use the micro-approach to regulate the accuracy of the rate of flow. Focus on the sounds that you create- they should be short, staccato and with a clear attack and definition. Pay attention to the velocity of each stroke.

USE METRONOME FOR ALL EXCERSICES AND COUNT OUT LOUD!
START SLOW, AND PRACTICE WITH INCREMENTS OF 2BPM/2MINS.

6.1 • Fundamental Sticking:

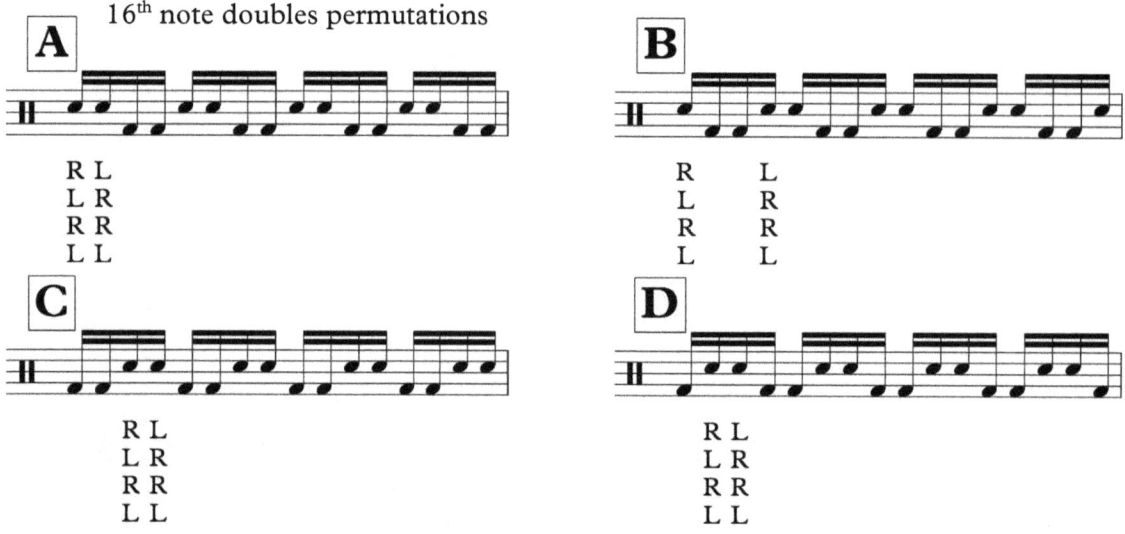

Work on each of the presented sticking possibilities for each permutation on snare and kick only. Once you can generate a consistent rate of flow and dynamic, start to combine sticking options.

6.2 • Orchestration:

Orchestrate and explore the stickings around the drum set with each one of the presented sticking for each permutation. Statistically, there are just too many ways to orchestrate this simple little pattern, and it would be overwhelming to go over all of them. The following examples are some of the most useful choices for orchestration and stickings. Make sure to explore more and find your sound.

6.2.1. Alternative Hand Patterns RL or LR

Examples are based on letter A; make sure to work through permutations B to D in the same manner.

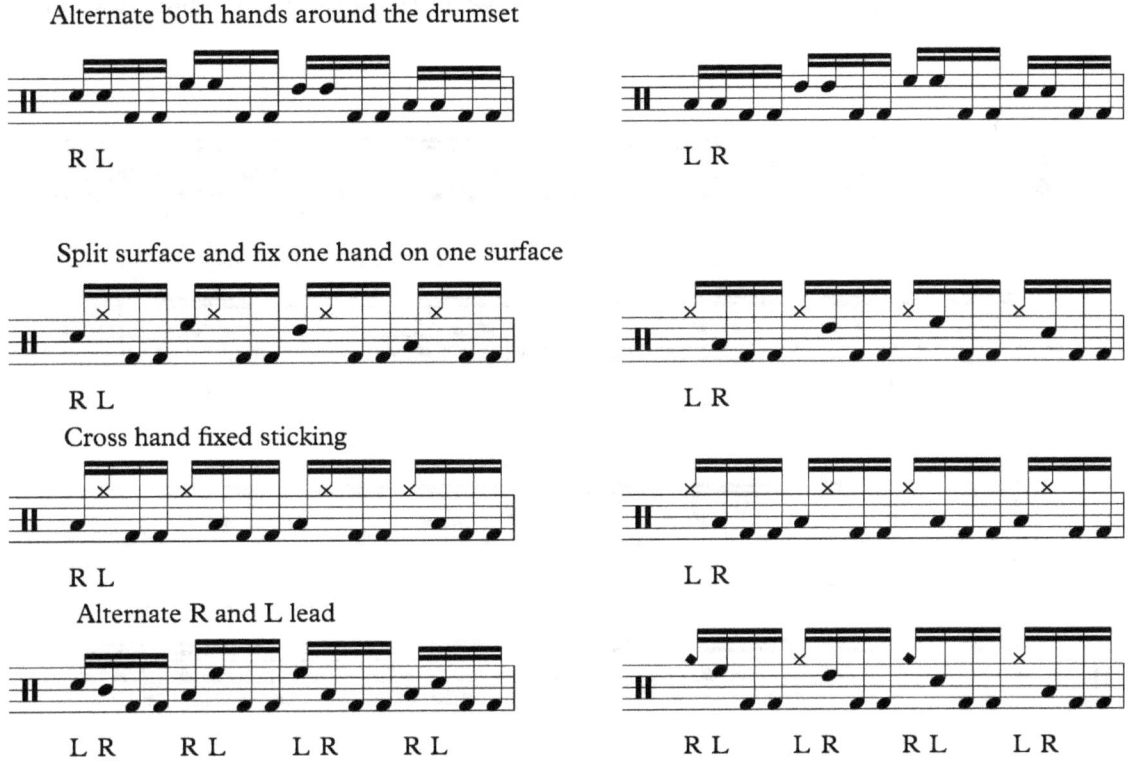

6.2.2. Double Stroke Sticking RR or LL

Examples are based on letter D; make sure to work through permutations A to C in the same manner.

Switch hand if you are left dominant or open-handed drummer.

6.3 • Grid:

The flow eventually becomes easier when one motion is adapted and repeated. Afterwards, you can break up the flow with a new motion to see how well we could eliminate the glitches at the transition points. Lastly, orchestrate the grid.

6.4 • Accents and Highlights:

6.4.1. Accents in Doubles

Adding accents to double strokes is very useful in many situations. Ghosting around the accents is sometimes tricky but rewarding.

An Analytical Approach to Linear Applications | 77

Ghosting after rimshot accent

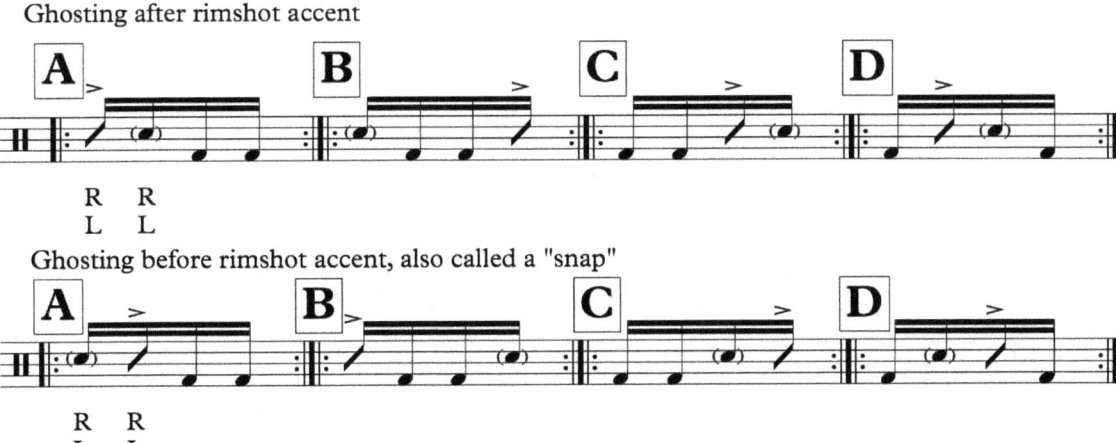

Ghosting before rimshot accent, also called a "snap"

6.4.2. FLAMS IN ALTERNATIVE STROKES

Adding accents to alternative stroking is very commonly used and is an advanced way to add more aggressive sonic characteristics and colors by adding flams to highlight the accent. *

Flammed Rimshot on the First Note of the Doubles

Flammed "Snap" on the Second Note of the Doubles

*If the accents are isolated out, the remaining parts are just the ghosted applications in exercise **6.2.2**.

6.4.3. Flams in Double Strokes

Flammed Rimshot on the First Note of the Doubles

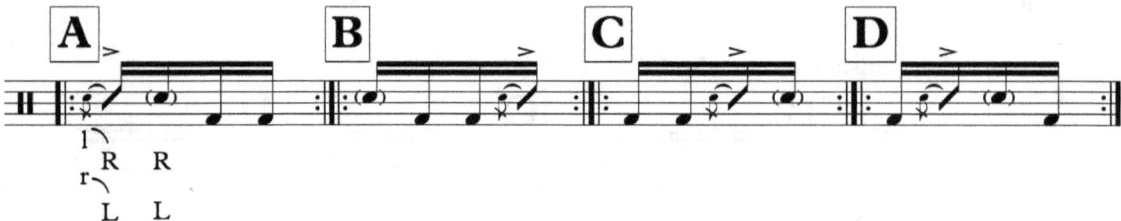

Flammed "Snap" on the Second Note of the Doubles

6.4.4. Double Flams

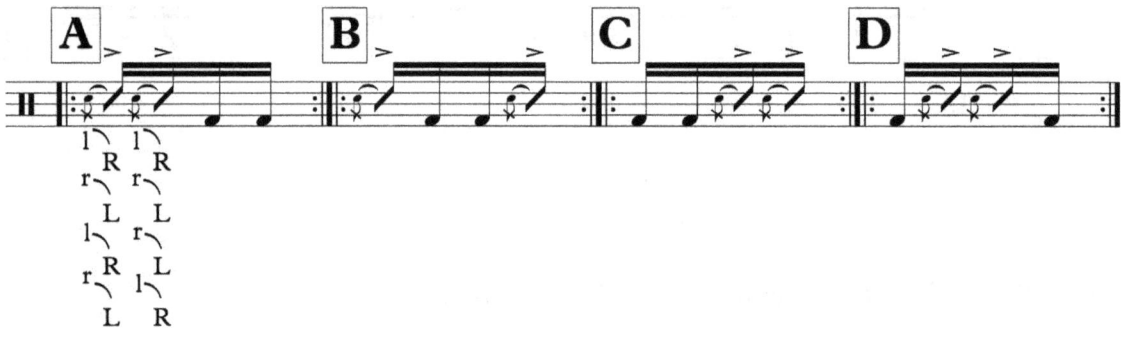

6.4.5. Orchestrating Flams

As demonstrated in letter A, work through permutations B to D.

The first way to orchestrate flams is based on  where the first of the doubles is accented.

The second way is based on  where the second note is accented. Notice that the rimshot on the snare is used as a flam in the third and fourth examples here.

The third way is to orchestrate the double flams in example 6.4.4 as follows.

6.4.6. Cymbal Highlights

As demonstrated in letter A, work through permutations B to D.

Now apply everything with the Grid for motion change workouts in 6.3.

An Analytical Approach to Linear Applications | 81

6.5• Rate Changing Grid:

Follow the A and B rate-changing grid; apply all the previous exercises into it. We are only using pattern A in the grid here, which should be substituted by permutations B to D once you have mastered the original pattern A. Work through the rate-changing grid with:

1. All stickings
2. All permutations
3. Accents and highlights
4. All permutations with accents and highlights

Use the metronome wisely.

SESSION 7

Linear Coordination Part 2: Single-Note Interdependence

Last session, we focused on double-note interdependence and ways to orchestrate it. In this session we will move our focus on to the single note interdependence, which is another key fundamental element of coordination patterns. Alternative singles in a linear fashion are more difficult to execute due to the faster rate of limbs switch, and this session is aimed to eliminate the transition glitches.

USE THE METRONOME FOR ALL EXCERCISES AND COUNT OUT LOUD!
START SLOW, AND PRACTICE WITH INCREMENTS OF 2BPM/2MINS.

84 | *Lang Zhao*

7.1• FUNDAMENTAL STICKING:

Alternative stroking is not as simple as it seems to be. It takes a longer time to develop a stable muscle memory with accuracy and consistency due to the fast rate of change of motion. You may commonly find that when starting an alternative singles pattern; the first couple cycles fluctuate and then begin to settle down and stabilize after a while. Therefore, it is vitally necessary to intentionally work on breaking up the repetition of patterns and starting new cycles to force you to adapt to the changes as quickly as possible. Follow the grid below to work through all the stickings.

7.1.1. FUNDAMENTAL STICKING

Original Singles

Alternative Singles between Hands and Foot

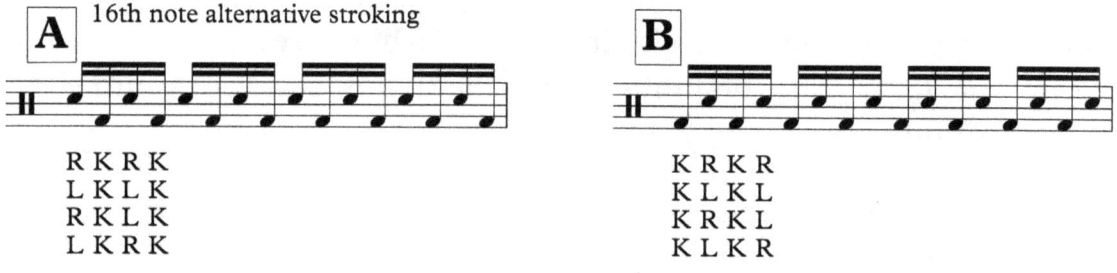

An Analytical Approach to Linear Applications | 85

7.1.2. Grid for Fundamental Stickings

Letter A (below) shows the switch between alternative hand strokes and alternative hand/foot strokes. Letter B (below) shows the switch between alternative hand strokes and alternative foot/hand strokes.

Swap circles 1 and 2 for the repeat. In letter A, circled numbers only represent 16th note passages. In letter B, circle 1 represents hand-leading passages, and circle 2 represents foot-leading passages.

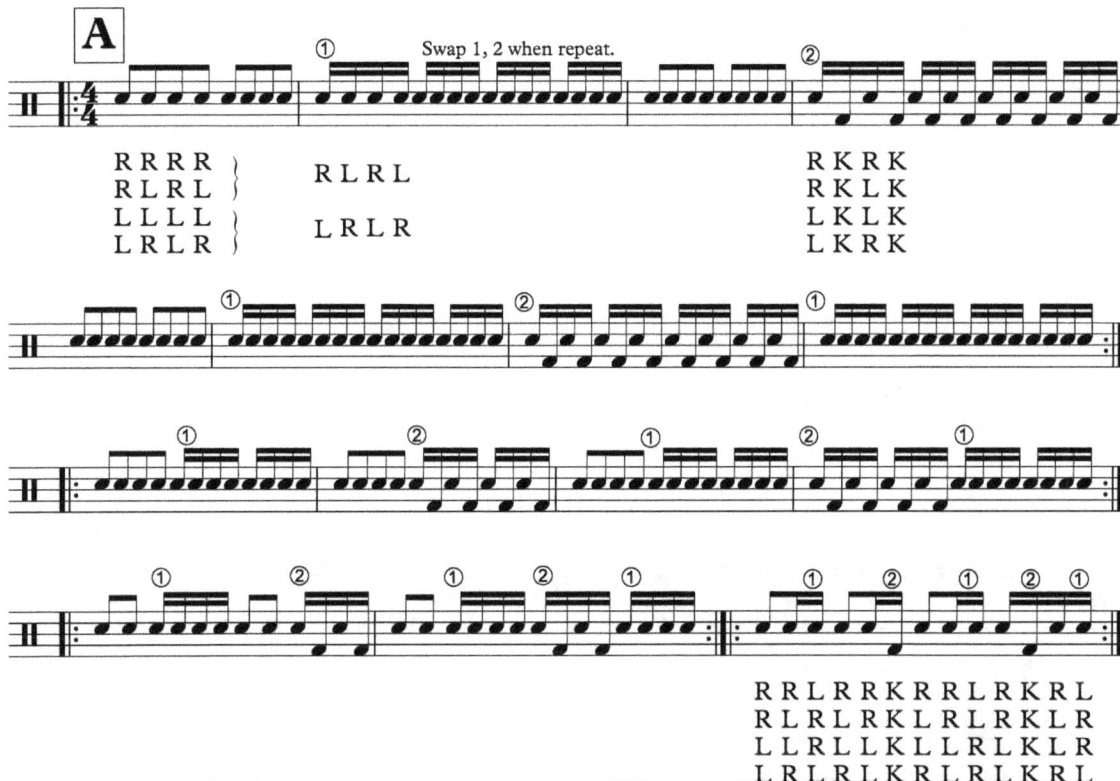

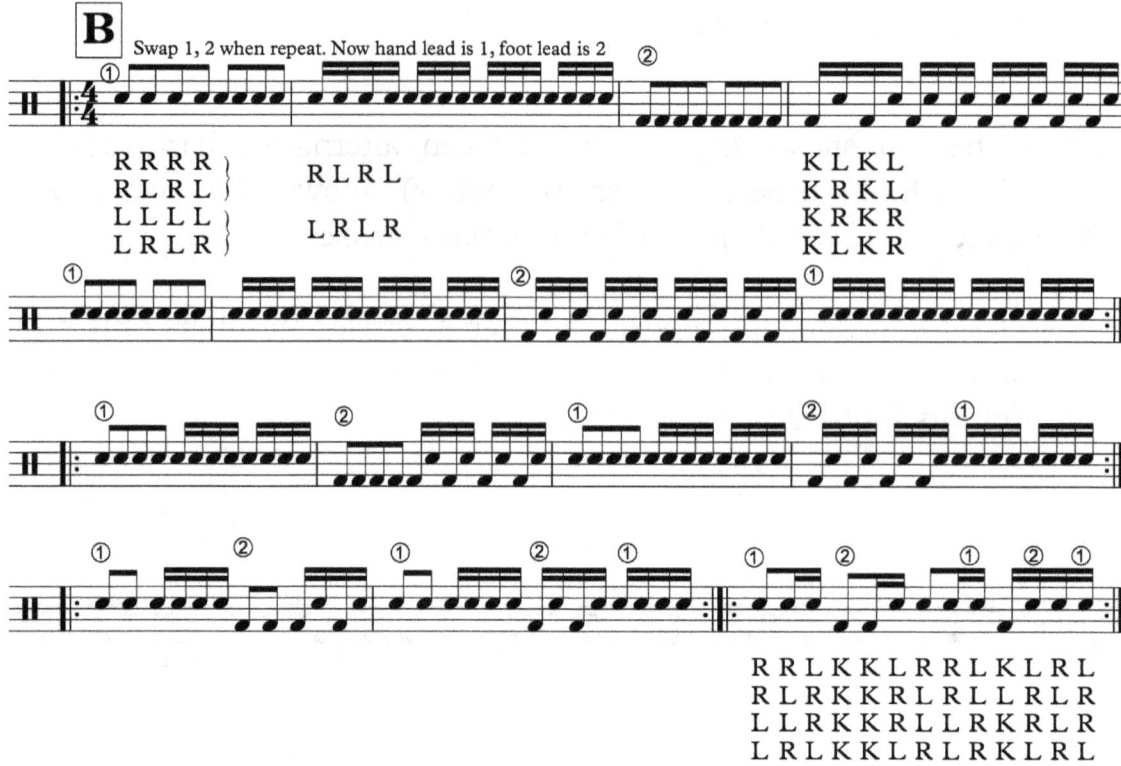

In letter C the rate is toggling between 16th note and sextuplets. Make sure you are not rushing the sextuplets.

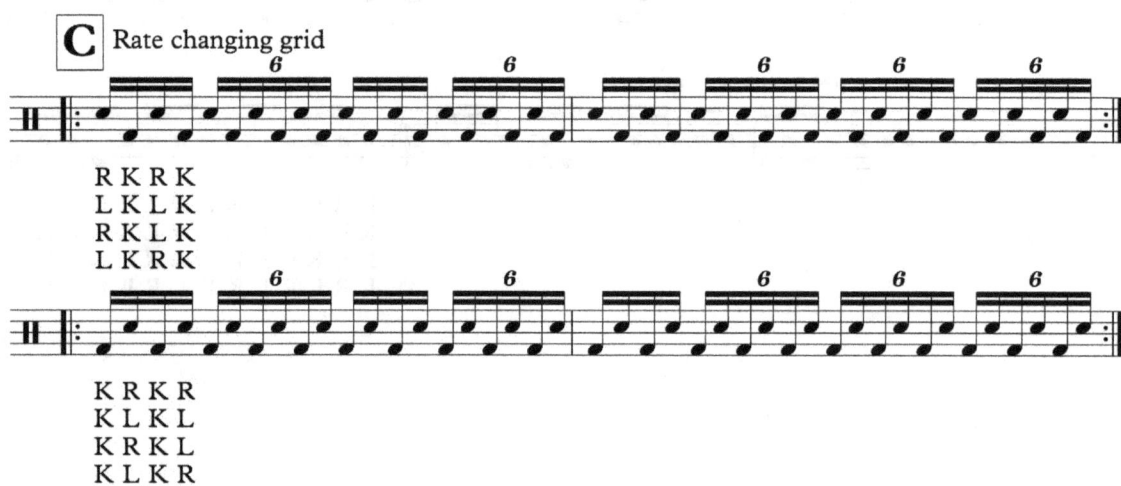

7.2 • BASIC GROUPINGS:

This exercise includes some of the most useful grouping ideas with single bass drum stroke. Work on each of the variations individually then apply them to the universal grid for EX 7.2.

7.2.1. FOUR-NOTE GROUPING

Bass Drum Placement Permutation

```
R  L  R  K
L  R  L  K
```

a. Work on each of the permutations individually.

b. Use the accent pattern provided below to apply accents. The example uses letter A for the fundamental stickings; go through permutation B to permutation D in the same manner. Use all the sticking patterns provided.

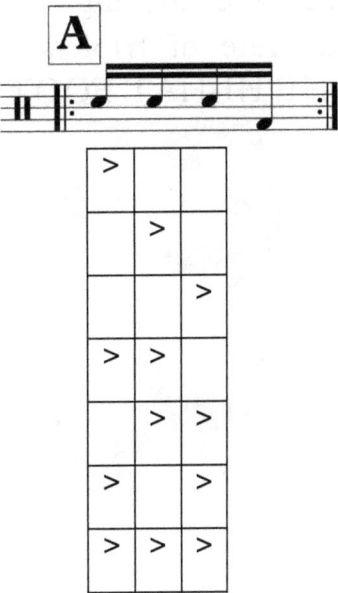

c. Follow the same accent grid above and apply flams as accents.

d. Apply all that you have worked on so far to the universal grid below.
   - Choose one accent pattern at a time to go over the grid first.
   - Mix up choices of accent patterns.

e. Orchestrate around the drum set.

f. Follow the Over-the-barline Grid below, apply one sticking pattern at a time; make sure you keep the sticking when you play the implied four-note grouping in the rate of triplets. KEEP THE QUARTER NOTE PULSE WITH THE HI-HAT FOOT!

An Analytical Approach to Linear Applications | 89

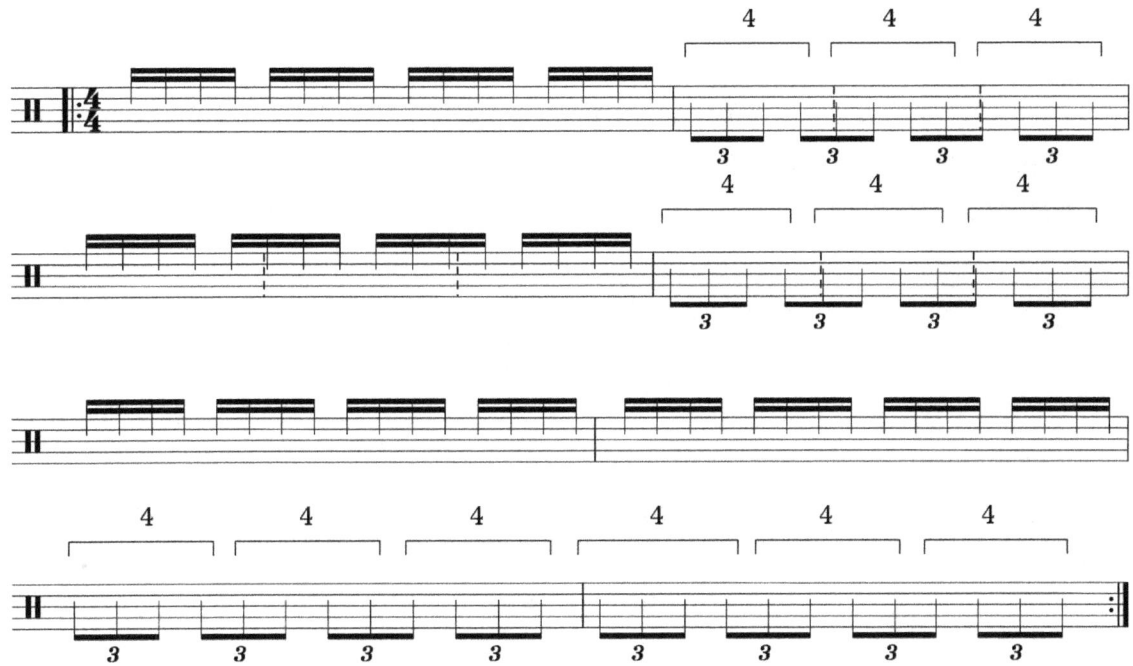

Example:

7.2.2. Three-Note Groupings

Bass Drum Permutation and Stickings

a. Work on each of the permutations individually.

b. Use the accent pattern provided below to apply accents. The example uses letter A of the fundamental stickings; go through permutation B to permutation D in the same manner. Use all the sticking patterns provided.

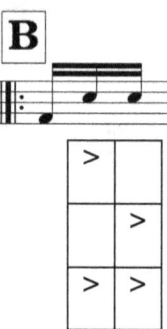

c. Follow the same accent grid above and apply flams as accents.

d. Apply all you have worked on so far to the universal grid below.
   - Choose one accent pattern at a time to go over the grid first.
   - Mix up your choices of accent patterns.

e. Orchestrate around the drum set.

f. Follow the Over-the-barline Grid below and apply one sticking pattern at a time; make sure you keep the sticking to play the implied three-note groupings in the rate of the 16th note. KEEP THE QUARTER NOTE PULSE WITH THE HI-HAT FOOT!!!

An Analytical Approach to Linear Applications | 91

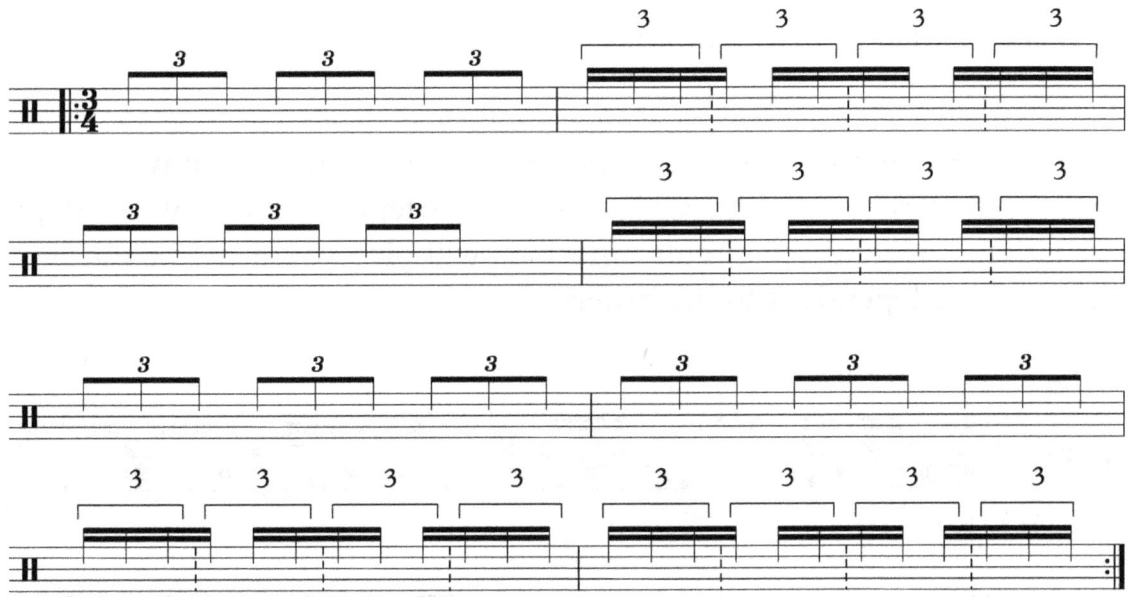

Example:

7.3 • Four-limb linear cycles workout:

This exercise contains two cycle motions among the four limbs—clockwise and counter-clockwise motion. Cross-limb interdependence is well adapted in most situations, while these circular motions will give you a better sense of how each limb is interdependent to the others.

SESSION 8

Groove Construction 1: The Paradiddle Series Rudiments

Paradiddles can be adapted seamlessly in linear playing. The nature of these rudiments makes them the most versatile in terms of application around the drum set in both grooves and chops. The combination of single and double strokes gives the paradiddle a natural two-layer dynamic and can help in turning around efficiently around the drums.

In last two sessions (6 and 7), we have examined the possible linear approaches to the doubles and alternative strokes, and worked through the heavy load of exercises to enhance the coordination of the limbs. Now it is time to move on and use that coordination to master the paradiddle-series-rudiment-based linear applications.

USE METRONOME FOR ALL EXCERSICES AND COUNT OUT LOUD!
START SLOW, AND PRACTICE WITH INCREMENTS OF 2BPM/2MIN.

8.1 • A List of Paradiddle Series on Snare Drum:

It is critical that you use a metronome to regulate the following rudiments. Keep everything at a consistent rate of flow and PAY EXTRA ATTENTION to the space between each note. QUALITY SHOULD ALWAYS COME BEFORE SPEED.

This is a review of the most common paradiddle series rudiments and their permutations. Please make sure to work with left hand lead sticking as well. Start slow at around 70 bpm. The goal is to feel the motion flow by implementing an accent for the first note of each bar and using your motion rather than overplaying the accent. Relax and use medium height, around 6" strokes first, to generate a full round sound then gradually lower the height to around 3" as speed increases. Try to keep the evenness except for the implemented accent, and watch out for consistency of rate and note placement accuracy.

After you go through them with your hands, use the hand-foot split index to work on the hand-foot interdependence.

1. Hand Split Index

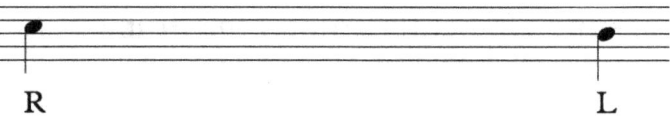

2. Hand Foot Split Index

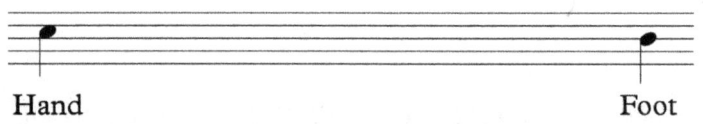

Apply both index 1 and 2 above to the following exercises.

An Analytical Approach to Linear Applications | 95

Double Paradiddle Permutation 2

Double Paradiddle Permutation 3

Double Paradiddle Permutation 4

Double Paradiddle Permutation 5

Paradiddle-diddle (right hand lead, make sure to work on left hand lead as well)

Paradiddle-diddle permutation 1

Paradiddle-diddle permutation 2

Paradiddle-diddle permutation 3

Paradiddle-diddle permutation 4

An Analytical Approach to Linear Applications | 97

Paradiddle-diddle permutation 5

Triple Paradiddle

Triple Paradiddle Permutation 1

Triple Paradiddle Permutation 2

Triple Paradiddle Permutation 3

Triple Paradiddle Permutation 4

Triple Paradiddle Permutation 5

Triple Paradiddle Permutation 6

Triple Paradiddle Permutation 7

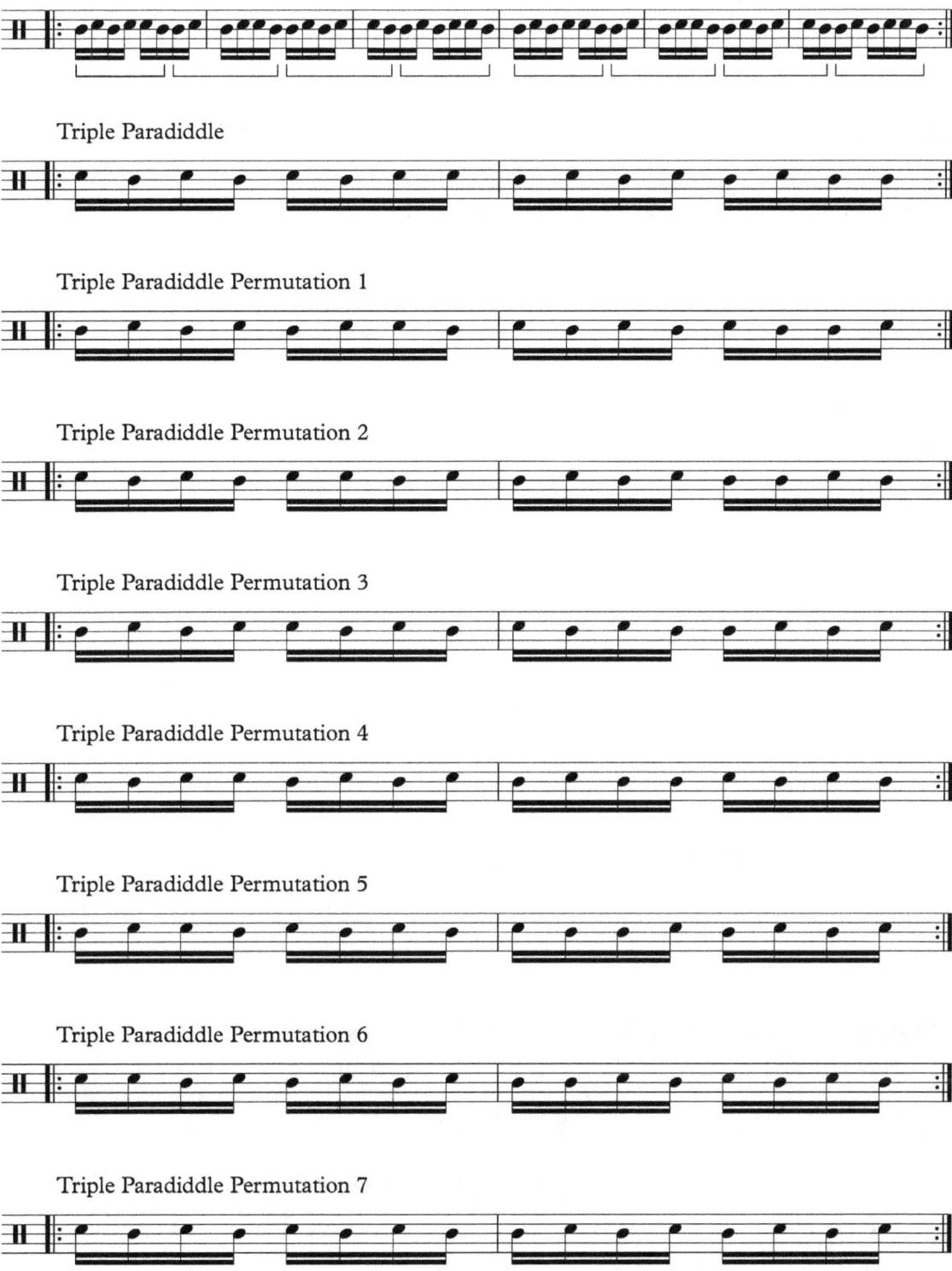

8.2 • Passive linear groove adaptation:

In this section, we will apply a simple orchestration to all the stickings above to transform them into grooves. The stickings will be split between hi-hat and snare since in contemporary music it is very practical that the core action be built upon the triangle of the kick, hat, and snare.

Before we start, let's recap the dynamic layers in Session 1, where we discussed the sound in detail.

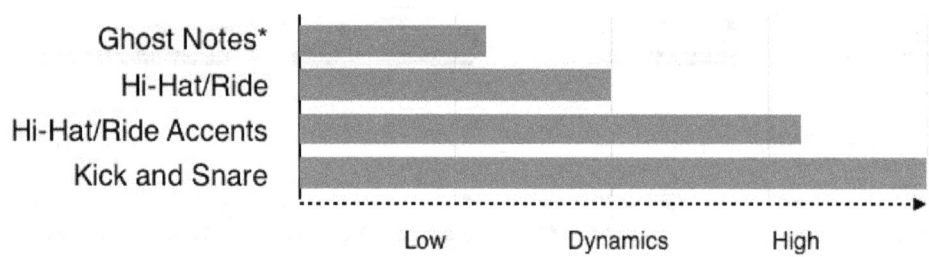

Ghost notes and unaccented hi-hat notes could be considered as having very similar sonic qualities, and they both serve as internal coherence to the groove. That's why dynamically they are in the same range. Paradiddle series rudiments could be broken up into these two sound sources to get a similar sound quality of ghost notes and unaccented hi-hat notes.

We will apply dual dynamic layers in the following manner:
    a. Accented notes are played with medium height 6" strokes.
    b. Unaccented notes are played with low height 3" strokes.

The clearer you can separate the dynamic layers, the better the punctuation will be. Be aware that the sound should be tight and staccato. Make sure you generate a good velocity at the moment you execute each stroke.

Step 1: Apply the previous Sound Index to the Original Drum Legend

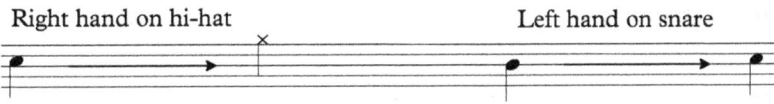

For example:

Step 2: Reading Figures Adaptation

A series of reading figures will be provided for you to merge into the orchestrated patterns in the last step. This step is a way to force the patterns into linear grooves for practice purposes.

When you see a figure like this being provided, for example:

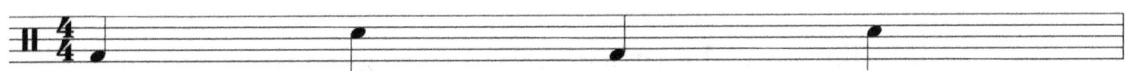

Let's say we choose to use single paradiddles as our sticking, and we swap the corresponding subdivision in the paradiddle to the reading figure:

All reading figures provided should be accented. They now become the primary layer in the groove. All the rest of the stickings should be treated as a subdominant layer, or as ghost notes.3

100 | *Lang Zhao*

Remember all snare accents should be as rimshots.

Let's look at another example:

Merge the following sticking and the reading figure:

Once your get familiar with the procedure, move on to the exercises. Please go over all the 27 paradiddle series stickings with the reading figures below. Not all stickings apply to the figures in the same effective way. Explore and choose which possible sticking you can take into practical applications.

8.3 • Workouts for Passive Linear Groove Adaptation:

EX 8.3.1: Basic Workout for Passive Linear Groove Adaptation

An Analytical Approach to Linear Applications | 103

EX 8.3.2: Half–Time Feel Workout for Passive Linear Groove Adaptation

EX 8.3.3: Applied 4-bar Phrase Exercise for Passive Linear Groove Adaptation

You may find that not all stickings presented will be practical to you; different individuals may have very different preferred stickings among all these possible applications. Don't be afraid to go over the awkward sticking situations; working on them as exercises will make you more fluent and confident when moving around the drums under any unexpected situation. Again, collect your favorite combinations and add them to your mastered drum vocabulary. Eventually you will develop your on ideas as to how to approach the musical content in a linear fashion.

SESSION 9

Hi-Hat Control

The hi-hat is the most expressive component in a drum set in terms of embellish your playing with a lot of colors. However, a lot of times, we almost forget about hi-hat control. During this chapter, we will briefly discuss some possible ways to manipulate the hi-hat.

9.1 • CLOSED HI-HAT:

- *Hand Stroke*

    o Be aware of the spot on the hi-hat you are hitting

    - The edge has the two pieces of cymbals contacting each other, which creates a rustling sound.
    - The more you move towards the bell, the more clicking sound you get.

- - Be aware of which part of the stick is creating contact with the hi-hat.

    - The shoulder creates a fatter sound. (Good for accents.)
    - When moving towards the tip, you will get a more defined attack and lighter tone. (Good for non-accents.)

- *Foot Steps*

  - How hard you step into the pedal controls the tightness of the closed hi-hat sound.

  - When generating a closed hi-hat sound with your foot, it creates a different sound than hitting it with the stick. It is closer to the sound creating while hitting by the shoulder of the sticks, but with a less aggressive and warmer tone.

9.2 • OPEN HI-HAT:

- *Hand Stroke*

  - Be aware of how much the hi-hat is open. The more open the hi-hat is, the washier it gets.

- *Foot Splash*

  - Foot splash creates a unique color that the stick cannot generate from contacting the hats. Foot splash creates a beautiful but less heavy ringing tone.

9.3 • OPEN/CLOSED HI-HAT:

- *Be specific about when to close the hi-hat, and how long the hats are kept opened.*

An Analytical Approach to Linear Applications | 107

The following exercises are created to review and check your awareness on hi-hat control. Please follow the instructions.

EX. 9.3.1: Closed Hi-Hat and Dual Dynamic Layers

In this exercise, use the shoulder of the stick to hit on the edge of the hat for the accents, and use the tip to hit the top hat for the non-accents. Focus on the consistency of the two dynamic layers and the accuracy of note placement. The hi-hat foot should apply proper pressure to get a tighter sound but still maintaining a good body balance. Feel the motion that connects the two different strokes.

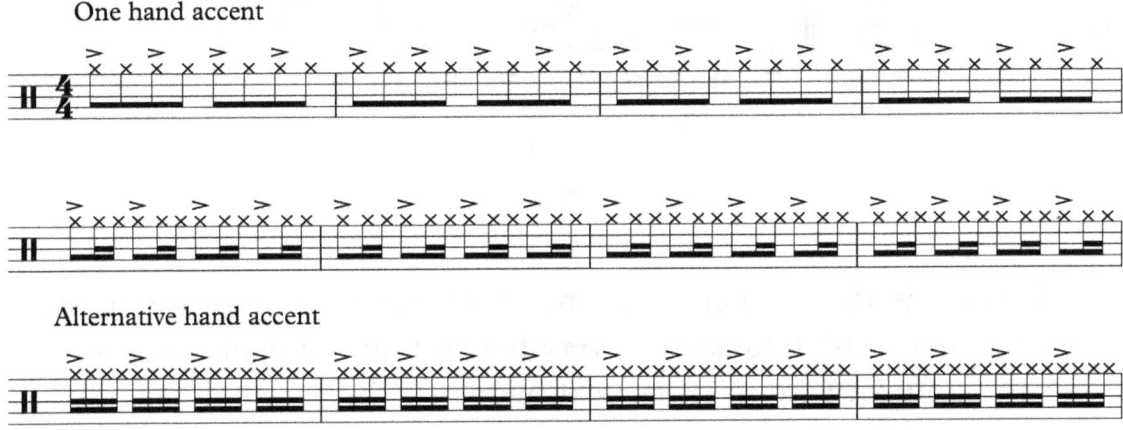

EX. 9.3.2: Recognize Foot Pressure

Gradually open and close the hi-hat with the control of foot while playing 16th notes with hands. Feel the different results while the hi-hat foot pressure changes.

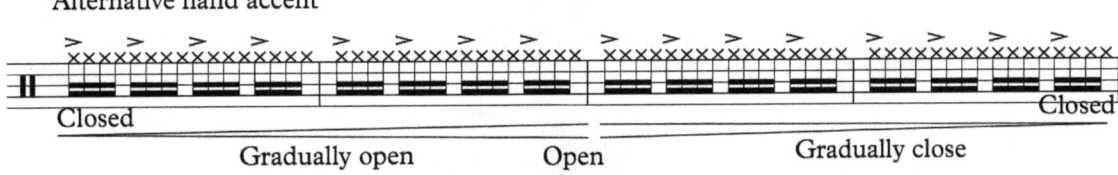

EX. 9.3.3: Hi-Hat Opening Duration

Below are some common situations of controlling hi-hat opening duration at certain subdivisions. Make sure you could execute them accurately.

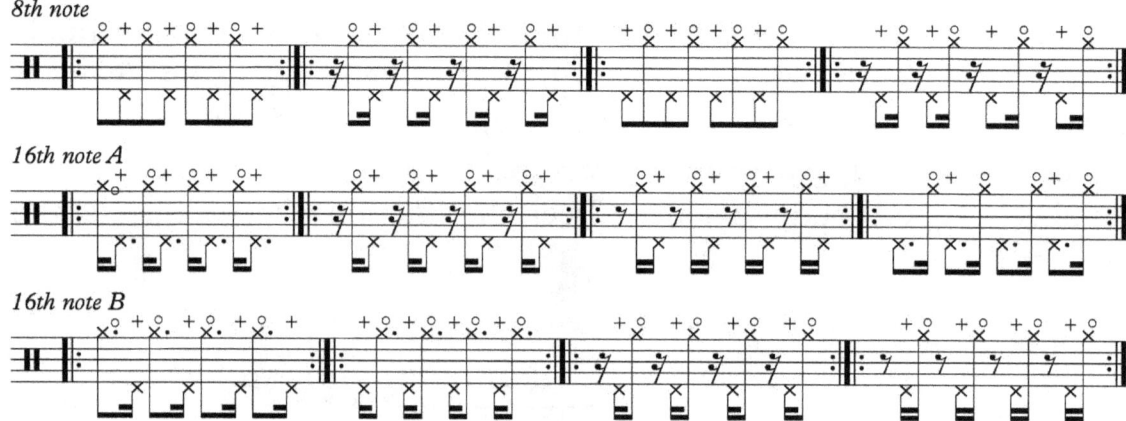

EX. 9.3.4: Permutations

The following is the 15 permutations of the groove in the first bar. Each permutation shifts a 16th note ahead every bar so that the open and closed hi-hat move one 16th note forward in every next bar as well.

Original groove with 8th note hi-hat open duration

Original groove with 16th note hi-hat opening duration

SESSION 10

Groove Construction 2: Dual Dynamic Layers Workout

In this session, we will continue to work on linear groove construction and using dynamic layers in these exercises. Again the main layer is the skeleton and the subdominant layer, or the lower dynamic layer, embellishes the skeleton using ghost notes. Make sure that you use metronome wisely with both the micro and the macro-approach to work on accuracy, consistency, timing and feel.

Instructions:

Everything happens here is within the kick-hat-snare triangle.

1. Follow the three series of figures (on the next page) featuring

    a. 8th note placements in 4/4 (1A, 1B)
    b. 16th note subdivision "e" and "a" in 4/4 (2A, 2B)
    c. 16th note two-note grouping placements in 4/4 (3A, 3B, 3C)
2. Use bass drum to read the figures, and apply the following:

    a. snare backbeat on "2" and "4" regular time feel
    b. snare backbeat on "3" half time feel
    c. swing the 16th note

3. If there is a figure overlapping the corresponding subdivision already (on "2" and "4" or "3"), then keep the snare backbeat and omit the bass drum.

4. Fill the blanks with the subdominant layer of hi-hat, and snare ghost notes in linear fashion. You don't need to follow the strict sticking rules in the paradiddle series session, but the object is to embellish the groove's skeleton with your mastered stickings instantly. The challenge is that the reading figures maintain change rather than a constant, so you have to focus to achieve a better mind-body connection and think quickly.

5. Then, use the same manner to work on the provided reading figures in other meters (4A.4B.4C).

6. Start slowly to get used to the process; establish the mind-body connection; focus on accuracy and consistency of note placement; maintain a good tone quality as we discussed before. We are looking for that staccato, full, clean tone with definition at any dynamic level. Pay attention to your stick control so that you can execute the two sticking heights in the dual dynamic layers. (3" and 6")

An Analytical Approach to Linear Applications | 113

The three series of figures (rehearse both straight and swung 16th note)

Lang Zhao

1B-1

1B-5

1B-9

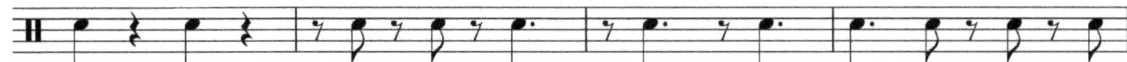

1B-13

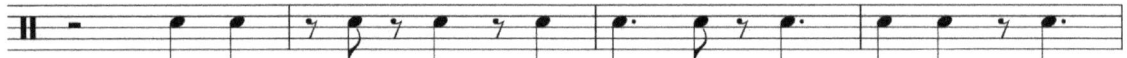

1B-17

1B-21

1B-25

1B-29

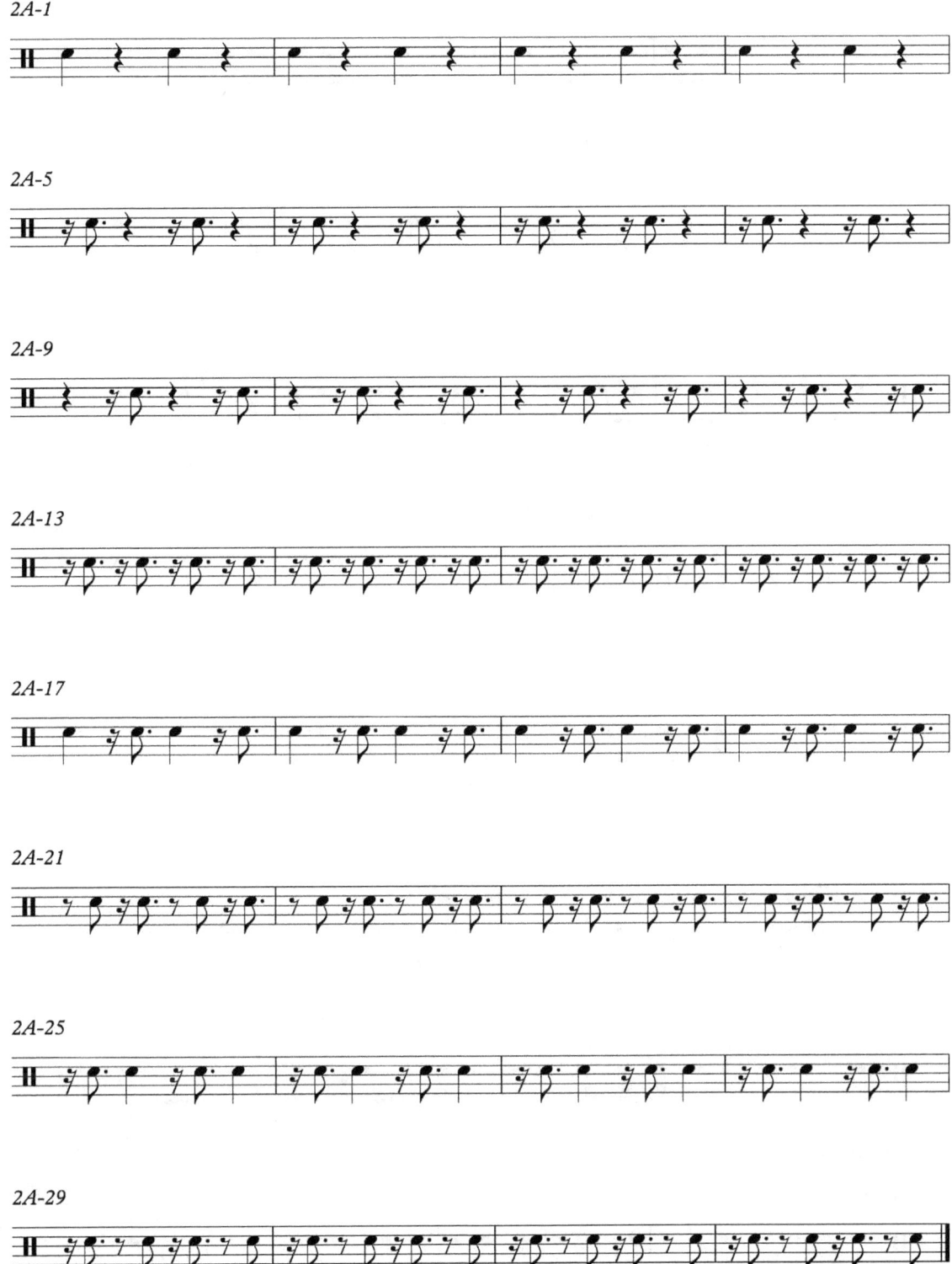

116 | Lang Zhao

2B-1

2B-5

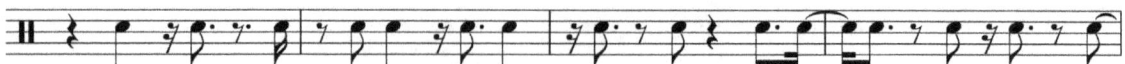

2B-9

2B-13

2B-17

2B-21

2B-25

2B-29

An Analytical Approach to Linear Applications | 117

3A-1

3A-5 Half time feel only

3A-9

3A-13

3A-17

3A-21

3A-25

3A-29

Lang Zhao

3B-1

3B-5

3B-9

3B-13

3B-17

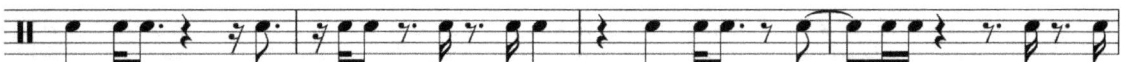

3B-21

3B-25

3B-29

Other Time Signatures

Snare backbeat on "1" of all the even number bars

Snare backbeat on "1" of even number bars or follows the split of 5 in 3+2 or 2+3

Snare backbeat on "1" of even number bars, or follow the groupings of 3+4 or 4+3

SESSION 11

Sonic Vocabulary and Chops Construction

Vocabulary is the listing of words someone knows or uses. In music, it is the range of possible features, effects or actions. We can define sticking vocabulary as the sticking patterns and phrases one can play.

11.1 • SONIC VOCABULARY:

Traditionally, you would use a sticking on a single surface and start to recognize the basic sonic effect of the sticking. Then you would orchestrate or change the rate around the drum set to further explore the sonic possibilities. But a lot of times you don't know what it would sound like until you play that sticking in a certain way; in other words, you might not be conscious of what is coming up next. During this last chops construction session, we will start from the sonic possibilities and look at possible ways of supporting them with sticking patterns.

These sonic possibilities you hear in your head before executing on drums could be referred to as your sonic vocabulary. Similar to how we defined the meaning of vocabulary earlier, sonic vocabulary is the range of possible sonic effects that you can hear, know or use.

To express sonic vocabulary freely, you need first to have a repertoire of stickings and be able to use them freely.

The below shows the differences between the sticking vocabulary approach and the sonic vocabulary approach when constructing chops:

Sticking Vocabulary	Sonic Vocabulary
Sound result is limited to sticking flow, different maneuvers on the drums lead to different results	Sound result is outlined already; different maneuvers only become embellishments
More mechanical and mathematical	More musical and organic
Serves as a tool	Functions as goals

We should always keep in mind that stickings are tools we use to achieve our sonic goals. The next session provides an example on how to work on constructing chops through the use of sonic vocabulary.

11.2 • CASE STUDY: CHOPS ANALYSIS—FACTORIZATION:

This is Letter G from Henry's demonstration transcription, in which there is a 16-bar improvised long passage of chops. In this case study, the passage of chops will be analyzed to see how it could be constructed and reproduced. Listen to it first without the transcription.

Letter G (00:02:59)

1. Two Dynamic Layers: Melodic vs. Subdominant

This 16-bar passage flows in 16th note subdivisions. It is not hard to find out that there are two dynamic layers after you listen to it carefully. One significant layer is the accented melody around the drum set, and the other layer consists of a lot of soft notes that flow around those accented melodies of the first layer. The melodic layer is accented with toms, bass drum, and snare drum rim shots, while the subdominant layer is embellishing the melodic layer with ghost notes and a closed hi-hat whose sonic qualities are similar.

2. Factorization of the Melodic Layer

Let's separate the melodic layer out from the passage by taking away the subdominant layer of soft notes.

Now the melodic layer is clearly shown, and you can see the orchestrated syncopation patterns in the melody. By observing the sonic vocabulary that Henry used to construct the melody, it is not hard to find out that there are some common styles of sound patterns appearing above the passage; for example, the combination of "e+", "e+a", "+a", etc. Clap the quarter note pulse and sing the melodic layer in your head.

128 | Lang Zhao

3. Factorizing out the One Voice Syncopation Rhythm.

One further step is taken here to show the rhythm's skeleton by itself; the melodic line is factorized down to just the rhythm.

Now listen to the passage again and clap the melodic rhythm with your hands only and see how it matches up with Henry's demonstration.

4. Sticking Vocabulary Involved

Listen to the interpretation of Letter G again and observe the sticking patterns. Try to connect the melody and the sticking patterns. From the observation, it is not hard to tell that the sticking vocabulary is from the paradiddle series and orchestrated around the drum set with highlights using flams and cymbals as we have discussed before. When you are physically accurate and fluent with the sticking patterns, they should come naturally after the sonic vocabulary has been heard or recognized.

EX 1

Study the sticking patterns in Letter G. Answer the following questions:

1. What rudiments are involved?

2. How is the kick drum added into the rudiments in the process of orchestration? What does it substitute?

3. How does the sticking vocabulary serve the sonic vocabulary?

11.3 • Sonic Vocabulary Workout Routine:

In this section, an effective way of practicing chops is introduced by reversing the process discussed in the case study above.

1. Create a rhythmic outline. For example, you initiated a four-bar phrase with the following rhythmic elements:

2. Hear a possible orchestration for the melody, for instance:

3. Sing the orchestrated melody until you internalize it. Then accordingly, apply sticking vocabulary to embellish the orchestrated melody. Here you need to think about how to treat the spaces; you could either leave them blank or connect them with some subdominant layer with ghost notes. The goal is to create a continuous 16th note flow that goes along with the melody.

4. Naturally, the stickings could be chosen and applied in the following manner.

5. When you do this exercise often enough, you should be able to freely come up with the similar type of syncopated orchestrated melody around the drums, and use your paradiddle series sticking vocabulary to fill up the spaces. Now let`s look into a different way to construct chops on top of the same melody, but with more advanced stickings like flams, hertas, drags, hi-hat accents, and rate changes.

IMPORTANT: USING THE ELEMENTS FROM THE MUSICAL CONTENT IS A WISE AND SAFE MANNER TO START WITH. DO NOT CHOP UNCONSCIOUSLY JUST BY LAYING DOWN STICKINGS. HUMBLY SERVE THE MUSIC AND ENJOY THE MOMENT!!!

EX 2: Chops Construction Stage 1—With Orchestrated Melody

The purpose of the stage 1 workout is to help expand your sonic vocabulary. Exercises are provided in various styles, and the melodies are already orchestrated. Sing each line with the metronome first and then apply your stickings to the melody with the provided subdivision. All stage 1 workouts are in 4-bar phrases. Remember you have the option to leave spaces.

The first line is the content, the second line is the orchestrated melodic skeleton accordingly; the third line is for you to construct chops on top of the melodic skeleton in the second line. Write down the sticking selections as a tool to embellish the sonic vocabularies.

Gospel

An Analytical Approach to Linear Applications | 133

Hip-hop

Stickings

Linear Fusion

Stickings

134 | *Lang Zhao*

Stickings

Stickings

An Analytical Approach to Linear Applications | 135

Stickings

EX 3: Chops Construction Stage 2—with Un-Orchestrated Melody Rhythmic Outline

In this part, only a rhythmic outline is provided. You will need to orchestrate and create chops on top of it.

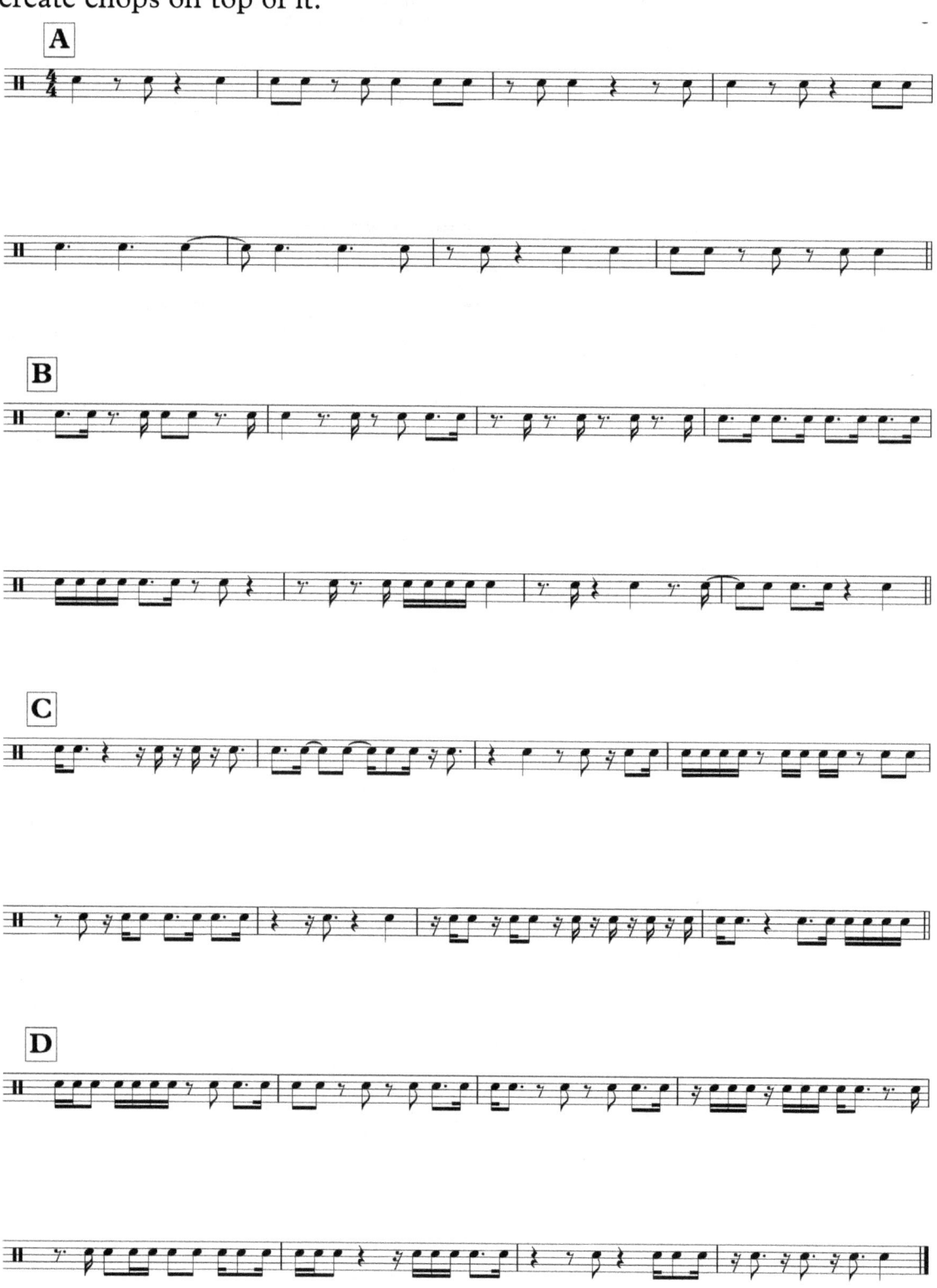

Please refer to the classic drum book New Breed I & II by Gary Chester for some similar figure reading exercises.

EX 4: Chops Construction Stage 3—with more Spaces to be filled up

Construct 8-bar phrases. Create a 4-bar phrase linear groove and follow up with some 4-bar phrase chops.

In this exercise, the provided figures are simpler and with more spaces; this means you won't get an orchestrated melody or detailed rhythmic outline anymore, but only the key figures. You will need to setup all the figures applying everything we discussed above. Remember to take the following aspects into consideration:

a. Melodic skeleton
b. Subdominant layer
c. Flams and cymbal highlights
d. Silent spaces in groove and chops
e. Changing rate (use such as 8th note, 8th note triplets, sextuplets, quintuplets, etc.)

An Analytical Approach to Linear Applications | 139

Sample @140bpm
Groove Sonic Vocabulary

Now use the same routine to work on the following exercises, following the instructions of indicated style, tempo and feel.

Instructions:

Over the bar-line fusion @155bpm with half-time feel

Groove sonic vocabulary

Chops sonic vocabulary

An Analytical Approach to Linear Applications | 141

Instructions:

Swung 16th note Funky R&B @95bpm, build chops with 16th note triplet subdivisions.

Groove sonic vocabulary

Chops sonic vocabulary

142 | *Lang Zhao*

Instructions:

16th note funky fusion @135bpm. Can you recognize where these rhythms come from? (hint: a baby dog that barks)

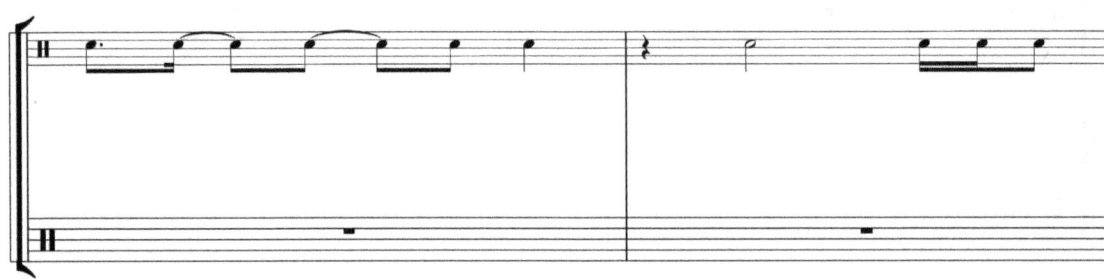

11.4 • REVIEW:

Now let's look at the demo tune "Drive It" again along with a little analysis on what is happening in the music.

DRIVE IT

Track by Kaz Rodriguez
Drums interpreted by Henry McDanel IV
As transcribed and analyzed by Lang Zhao

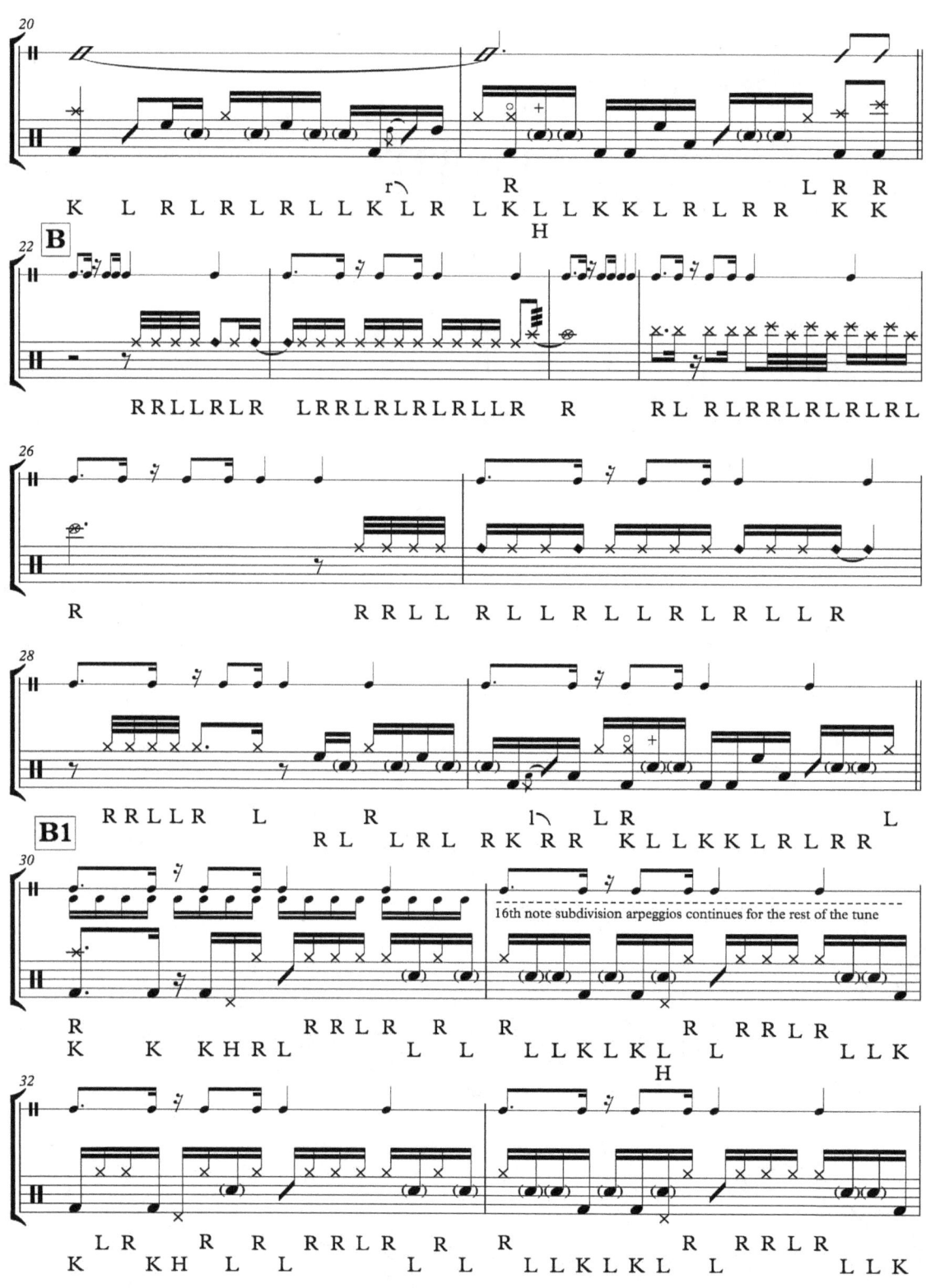

An Analytical Approach to Linear Applications | 145

146 | Lang Zhao

An Analytical Approach to Linear Applications | 147

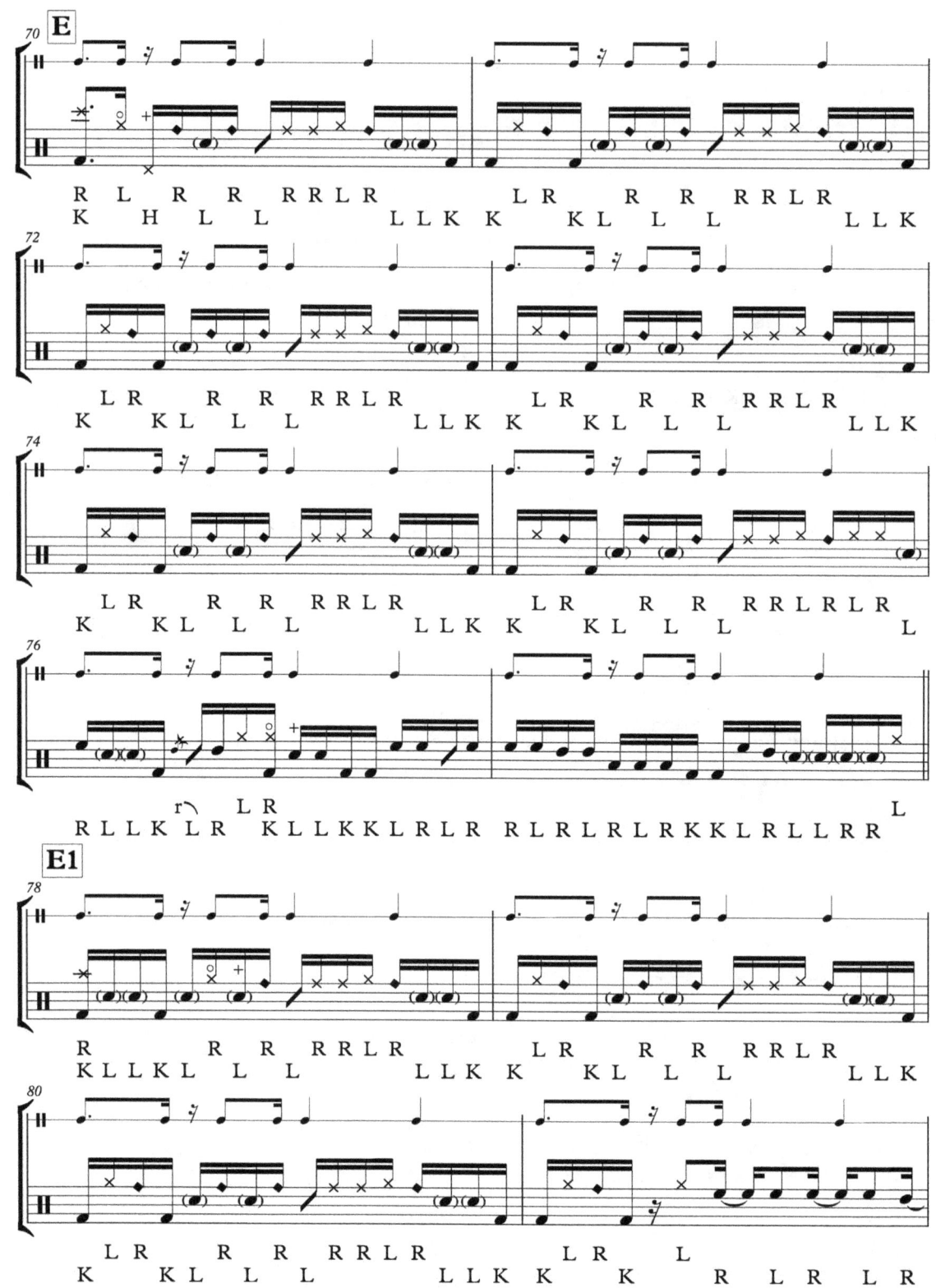

An Analytical Approach to Linear Applications | 149

150 | *Lang Zhao*

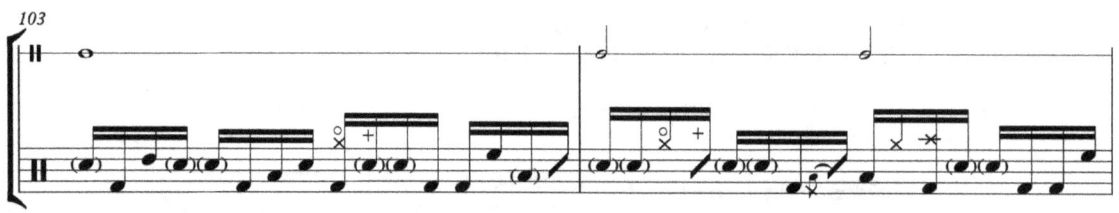

An Analytical Approach to Linear Applications | 151

It is now time for you to interpret this track and check what you have learned from this project. Feel free to incorporate all the ideas to your playing style in order to create something unique and valuable. Of course, things do not end here, and you can always to write out the melodies you hear and expand them to grooves and chops. The more you work on them in this manner, the more fluent you will be when translating what you hear onto the drums.

Conclusion

This is the end of the book.

Linear applications could be very useful and powerful at the right moments. Please take with you the analytical approach that we have used in the study; it will help you acquire new information more efficiently.

Different techniques are tools to enhance your relationship with your instrument and will help you speak better via your instrument. We practice mastering more tools so that we could use them to serve the music better. Creating good music is the ultimate goal.

This is the start of your new exploration.

For more information about this book and future releases, please visit www.langzhaomusic.com

Index

Accents, 12, 29, 64, 65, 69, 74, 75, 77, 87, 93, 94, 116
Backbeat, 44, 51, 99, 107, 108
Chops, 1, 7, 10, 18, 37, 44, 51, 53, 54, 55, 56, 57, 80, 109, 110, 115, 116, 117, 121, 122, 125, 136
Counting System, i, 27
Definition, 13, 14, 61, 99
Gears, 17
Ghost notes, 29, 44, 45, 52, 85, 86, 98, 99, 111, 115
Grid, 20, 64, 69, 71, 74, 75, 77
Hi-hat, 14, 24, 29, 44, 45, 48, 52, 55, 85, 92, 93, 94, 95, 99, 111, 116
Lnear, 7, 11, 18, 33, 34, 35, 36, 37, 44, 45, 49, 51, 55, 57, 70, 79, 80, 85, 86, 91, 98, 99, 122
Linear Applications, 2, i, 34, 35, 36
Linear Drumming, 18
Macroscope References, 28
Metronome, 7, 10, 14, 19, 20, 21, 22, 23, 24, 25, 26, 28, 29, 59, 61, 69, 81, 98, 117
Metronome System, i, 28
Microscope References, 28
Ostinato, 18, 35, 36, 44
Paradiddles, 80
Permutation, 62, 63, 67, 68, 69, 74, 77, 95
Practice, 26, 58, 59, 60, 86, 137
Rudiments, 59, 80, 81, 85, 114
Skeleton, 44, 45, 49, 50, 51, 53, 54, 55, 56, 57, 98, 99, 113, 117, 122
Sonic, 7, 12, 33, 45, 46, 47, 48, 50, 52, 54, 55, 56, 57, 65, 85, 109, 110, 111, 113, 114, 117
Staccato, 13
Sticking, 7, 46, 47, 50, 57, 62, 74, 75, 77, 81, 86, 87, 91, 99, 109, 110, 114, 115, 116, 117
Straight Counting, 27
Subdivision, 10, 20, 21, 22, 23, 24, 28, 29, 44, 45, 59, 86, 98, 99, 117, 125
Swung Counting, 27
Touch and Tone, 13
Velocity, 13, 26, 61, 85
Weight distribution, 16, 17

ABOUT THE AUTHOR

LANG ZHAO

Lang started to study piano at the age of 4 and orchestral percussion at 14.
A classical training brought him solid and effective foundational approaches to learning different instruments and music.

Before coming to the U.S., Lang participated in numerous provincial and national contests for both piano and drums in China, and was the winner and runner-up in most of them.

He also passed the top-level performance certificate exams from the Chinese Musicians Association, Central Conservatory and the Shanghai Conservatory, obtaining the top-level performance certification for both piano and drums.

In 2011, Lang obtained a Bachelor's Degree in B.A, Finance, from Ohio State University; however he decided to keep pursuing his dream in music.

After graduating, Lang moved to L.A. to attend Musicians Institute to further study drums. Here he received the 2013 Musicians Institute Outstanding Player Award. He was also featured at Drumchannel Live around that same time.

Lang went on to become a staff member at Musicians Institute afterwards. He stayed in L.A. to further research the art form of drumming and to study with/ receive mentorship from the drumming greats such as Rob Carson, Chuck Silverman, Matt Garstka, Gordon Campbell and many others.

The advantages from Lang's diverse cultural background and past experiences not only allowed him to become a versatile drummer, but also offered him very effective and efficient approaches to analyze and summarize information systematically from a very unique point of view.

Lang currently works as a drummer and composer. He is also working on a series of books on drumming that cover a variety of topics that range from playing technique to different styles, including research on gospel influenced drumming.

www.ingramcontent.com/pod-product-compliance
Lightning Source LLC
Chambersburg PA
CBHW062130160426
43191CB00013B/2256